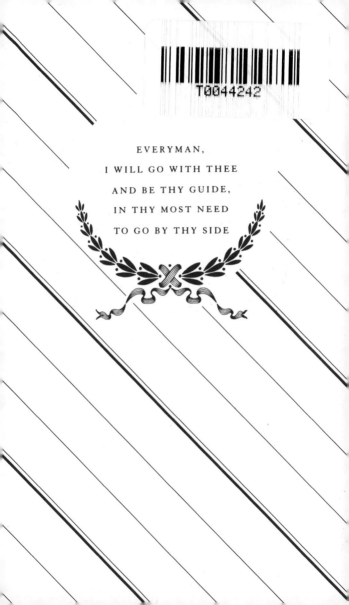

EVERYMAN,
I WILL GO WITH THEE
AND BE THY GUIDE,
IN THY MOST NEED
TO GO BY THY SIDE

EVERYMAN'S LIBRARY
POCKET POETS

IRISH
POEMS

••••••••••••••••••

EDITED BY
MATTHEW McGUIRE

EVERYMAN'S LIBRARY
POCKET POETS

Alfred A. Knopf New York London Toronto

THIS IS A BORZOI BOOK

PUBLISHED BY ALFRED A. KNOPF

This selection by Matthew McGuire first published in
Everyman's Library, 2011
Copyright © 2011 by Everyman's Library

Tenth printing (US)

A list of acknowledgments to copyright owners appears at the back
of this volume.

All rights reserved. Published in the United States by Alfred A. Knopf,
a division of Penguin Random House LLC, New York, and in Canada by
Penguin Random House Canada Limited, Toronto. Distributed by Penguin
Random House LLC, New York. Published in the United Kingdom by
Everyman's Library, 50 Albemarle Street, London W1S 4BD and
distributed by Penguin Random House UK,
20 Vauxhall Bridge Road, London SW1V 2SA.

www.randomhouse.com/everymans
www.everymanslibrary.co.uk

ISBN 978-0-307-59498-3 (US)
978-1-84159-786-7 (UK)

A CIP catalogue record for this book is available from the British Library

Typography by Peter B. Willberg

Typeset in the UK by AccComputing, North Barrow, Somerset

Printed and bound in Germany by GGP Media GmbH, Pössneck

CONTENTS

PLACE MATTERS

EXPERIENCE MATTERS

LOVE MATTERS

PREFACE

Out of the argument with others we make rhetoric; out of the argument with ourselves we make poetry. So said Ireland's most famous poet, W. B. Yeats. And it is poetry, rather than prose, that is seen as providing the most sustained and meaningful response to Ireland's turbulent history. From the romantic ballad to the rebel song, Irish poetry has been 'involved', to borrow a local euphemism, in mediating and mitigating histories of loyalty and loss. For some Irish writers poetry has been a place of self-reflection and self-doubt, a moment of quietude amid the deafening roar of partisan politics and all its bloody consequences. Argument, altercation, accommodation; the leitmotifs of many of the poems gathered in this volume. Over this aspect of Irish poetry preside the towering figures of William Butler Yeats and Seamus Heaney. Their most famous work emerged in response to the collapse of Irish society, Yeats during the aftermath of the 1916 Rising and Heaney during the outbreak of the Northern Irish Troubles in 1969. Ironically, if civil war made civil hands unclean, it also unearthed fertile ground for the poetic imagination. Under the heading of 'Political Matters' this book features attempts by Yeats, Heaney and others to interrogate the past, realize the present, and realign the co-ordinates of Ireland's future.

Dating back over fourteen hundred years, Irish poetry has its roots in two traditions: the devotional verse of the early Christian church and the long lyric poem of the bard, or *seanchaidhe*, that carrier of communal memory. Religion has always been part of Ireland's historical and cultural makeup, both a blessing and a curse, the pathway to another world and an obstacle on the road to renewal. Under the aegis of 'Religious Matters' this book features a number of attempts, both ancient and modern, to map the landscape of Ireland's theological inheritance.

'Gaelic Matters' turns its attention to that other vital source of Irish poetry, the Irish language. Up until the eighteenth century Irish poetry was primarily a Gaelic affair. The deep well of Gaelic culture, its steady decline and the catastrophic effects of the Irish famine all feature in this volume. There is an extract from Brian Merriman's eighteenth-century epic, *The Midnight Court*. The high point of modern Gaelic poetry, it is an epic masterpiece, deeply wrought and darkly comic. The book also features the interest in ancient Celtic myth, including the stories of Cuchulain and Deirdre, by various Anglo-Irish writers, not least W. B. Yeats himself.

One might be forgiven for thinking that Irish poetry is one long meditation in a time of civil war. The remaining sections of the book offer a welcome antidote to such mistaken notions. 'Place Matters' includes a diverse set of responses to the experience of the various Irish land-scapes, both rural and urban. It explores what it means to come from, and reside in, a particular place. 'Experi-ence Matters' charts the ways in which Irish writers, from the eighteenth century to the present day, deploy the rigours of poetic form to illuminate and transform the everyday world. 'Love Matters' concludes this selec-tion, recording an array of Irish responses to what is the most popular and recurrent theme in the whole of poetry.

Matt McGuire

RELIGIOUS
MATTERS

A BOAT SONG

The driving keel, cut from the forest – look – travels
    the current
of the twin-horned Rhine, and slides over the water
    like oil.
Together, men! Let the sounding echo return our cry.

The winds raise their breath, the harsh rain hurts us,
but men's proper strength prevails and drives off
    the storm.
Together, men! Let the sounding echo return our cry.

The clouds fade in time, and so the storm will yield.
Our efforts will tame it. Steady toil conquers all.
Together, men! Let the sounding echo return our cry.

Stand fast, and hold yourselves ready for better things.
You have suffered harder, and God will end even this.
Together, men! Let the sounding echo return our cry.

So the foul fiend works: he tires our hearts with fury,
and with evil temptation shakes our innermost hearts.
Keep Christ in your minds, my men, and let your cry
    re-echo.

Stay stern in your resolve, spurn the lures of the enemy
and seek your safety in the weapons of virtue.
Keep Christ in your minds, my men, and let your cry
re-echo.

Firm faith and a blessed zeal will conquer all.
The ancient enemy will fail and shatter his arrows.
Keep Christ in your minds, my men, and let your cry
re-echo.

The King of every good, the source, the height of
power,
gives promise as we strive, gives the prize when we
succeed.
Keep Christ in your minds, my men, and let your cry
re-echo.

MONASTIC POEM

All alone in my little cell
with no one for company,
I love this place of pilgrimage
now while I still have life.

A hut remote and hidden
for repenting of all sin,
with upright conscience, unafraid
in the face of holy Heaven.

With a body that good habits
made holy, treading it down,
and eyes worn out and tearful
with penance for my desires,

with weak, subdued desires
and denial of the wretched world,
with innocent, eager thoughts,
so let us sue to God.

With sincere lamentations
up to cloudy Heaven,
earnest devout confession,
intense tears in torrents;

on a cold, nervous bed
– as a doomed man might lie down –
with short, anxious sleep
and prayer early and often.

As to property and food
our one wish – to abstain.
For certain what I eat
will be no cause of sin:

dry bread measured out
with virtuous head bowed low,
and water from the bright hill
our proper draught to drink.

A salt and meagre diet
with mind bent on a book;
no disputation, visitation;
conscience serene and calm.

How wonderful it would be
– some pure and holy blemish,
cheeks dried and sunken in,
skin leathery and lean!

Christ, God's Son, to visit me,
my Maker and my King,
my spirit turning toward Him
and the Kingdom where He dwells.

And let the place that shelters me
behind monastic walls
be a lovely cell, with pillars pure,
and I there all alone.

A HERMIT'S SONG

My heart stirs quietly now to think
of a small hut that no one visits
in which I will travel to death in silence.

Nothing will draw my eyes away,
there, from repentance for evil done,
or hinder my view of Heaven and Earth.

Feeble and properly tearful, I'll pray
as the body decays, always treating it firmly
to serve only my soul there.

Passions, grown weak, will not divide me:
where they die the soul steps forward
eager to serve and seek for pardon.

I will have no ease nor long lying,
but short sleep, out on the edge of life,
and early waking for penance and long prayer.

Hardly a mile from this pleasant clearing
is a bright spring to drink from and use
for moistening measured pieces of bread.

For all my renouncing and sparse diet
and regular tasks of reading and penance
I foresee only delight in my days there.

The thinness of face and fading of skin,
the pain given by damp and a hard bed
to a frail body, will hardly distress me,

for I look to have frequent visits from birds
and sunlight and Jesus the King who made me,
and my mind will be calling on Him each morning.

When I and the things I used are faded,
some men will remember and respect the place
where a man all day prepared his dying.

ANON.

TRANS. JAMES SIMMONS

SAINT PATRICK'S BREASTPLATE

Today I put on
a terrible strength
invoking the Trinity,
confessing the Three
with faith in the One
as I face my Maker.

Today I put on the power
of Christ's birth and baptism,
of His hanging and burial,
His resurrection, ascension
and descent at the Judgment.

Today I put on the power
of the order of Cherubim,
angels' obedience,
archangels' attendance,
in hope of ascending
to my reward;
patriarchs' prayers,
prophets' predictions,
apostles' precepts,
confessors' testimony,
holy virgins' innocence
and the deeds of true men.

Today I put on
the power of Heaven,
the light of the Sun,
the radiance of the Moon,
the splendour of fire,
the fierceness of lightning,
the swiftness of wind,
the depth of the sea,
the firmness of earth
and the hardness of rock.

Today I put on
God's strength to steer me,
God's power to uphold me,
God's wisdom to guide me,
God's eye for my vision,
God's ear for my hearing,
God's word for my speech,
God's hand to protect me,
God's pathway before me,
God's shield for my shelter,
God's angels to guard me
from ambush of devils,
from vice's allurements,
from traps of the flesh,
from all who wish ill,
whether distant or close,
alone or in hosts.

I summon these powers today
to take my part against every implacable power
that attacks my body and soul,
the chants of false prophets,
dark laws of the pagans,
false heretics' laws,
entrapments of idols,
enchantments of women
or smiths or druids,
and all knowledge that poisons
man's body or soul.

Christ guard me today
from poison, from burning,
from drowning, from hurt,
that I have my reward,

Christ beside me,
    Christ before me,
        Christ behind me,

Christ within me,
    Christ beneath me,
        Christ above me,

Christ on my right hand,
    Christ on my left,

Christ where I lie,
   Christ where I sit,
      Christ where I rise,

Christ in the hearts of all who think of me,
Christ in the mouths of all who speak to me,
Christ in every eye that sees me,
Christ in every ear that hears me.

Today I put on
a terrible strength,
invoking the Trinity,
confessing the Three,
with faith in the One
as I face my Maker.

Domini est salus.
Domini est salus.
Domini est salus.
Salus tua, Domine, sit semper vobiscum.

PENAL LAW

Burn Ovid with the rest. Lovers will find
A hedge-school for themselves and learn by heart
All that the clergy banish from the mind,
When hands are joined and head bows in the dark.

ANK'HOR VAT

The antlered forests
Move down to the sea.
Here the dung-filled jungle pauses

Buddha has covered the walls of the great temple
With the vegetative speed of his imagery

Let us wait, hand in hand

No Western god or saint
Ever smiled with the lissom fury of this god
Who holds in doubt
The wooden stare of Apollo
Our Christian crown of thorns:
There is no mystery in the luminous lines
Of that high, animal face
The smile, sad, humouring and equal
Blesses without obliging
Loves without condescension;
The god, clear as spring-water
Sees through everything, while everything
Flows through him

A fling of flowers here
Whose names I do not know

Downy, scarlet gullets
Green legs yielding and closing

While, at my mental distance from passion,
The prolific divinity of the temple
Is a quiet lettering on vellum.

Let us lie down before him
His look will flow like oil over us.

LENT

Mary Magdalene, that easy woman,
Saw, from the shore, the seas
Beat against the hard stone of Lent,
Crying, 'Weep, seas, weep
For yourselves that cannot dent me more.

'O more than all these, more crabbed than all stones,
And cold, make me, who once
Could leap like water, Lord. Take me
As one who owes
Nothing to what she was. Ah, naked.

'My waves of scent, my petticoats of foam
Put from me and rebut;
Disown. And that salt lust stave off
That slavered me – O
Let it whiten in grief against the stones

'And outer reefs of me. Utterly doff,
Nor leave the lightest veil
Of feeling to heave or soften.
Nothing cares this heart
What hardness crates it now or coffins.

'Over the balconies of these curved breasts
I'll no more peep to see
The light procession of my loves
Surf-riding in to me
Who now have eyes and alcove, Lord, for Thee.'

'Room, Mary,' said He, 'ah make room for me
Who am come so cold now
To my tomb.' So, on Good Friday,
Under a frosty moon
They carried Him and laid Him in her womb.

A grave and icy mask her heart wore twice,
But on the third day it thawed,
And only a stone's-flow away
Mary saw her God.
Did you hear me? Mary saw her God!

Dance, Mary Magdalene, dance, dance and sing,
For unto you is born
This day a King. 'Lady,' said He,
'To you who relent
I bring back the petticoat and the bottle of scent.'

DESERTMARTIN

At noon, in the dead centre of a faith,
Between Draperstown and Magherafelt,
This bitter village shows the flag
In a baked absolute September light.
Here the Word has withered to a few
Parched certainties, and the charred stubble
Tightens like a black belt, a crop of Bibles.

Because this is the territory of the Law
I drive across it with a powerless knowledge –
The owl of Minerva in a hired car.
A Jock squaddy glances down the street
And grins, happy and expendable,
Like a brass cartridge. He is a useful thing,
Almost at home, and yet not quite, not quite.

It's a limed nest, this place. I see a plain
Presbyterian grace sour, then harden,
As a free strenuous spirit changes
To a servile defiance that whines and shrieks
For the bondage of the letter: it shouts
For the Big Man to lead his wee people
To a clean white prison, their scorched tomorrow.

Masculine Islam, the rule of the Just,
Egyptian sand dunes and geometry,
A theology of rifle-butts and executions:
These are the places where the spirit dies.
And now, in Desertmartin's sandy light,
I see a culture of twigs and bird-shit
Waving a gaudy flag it loves and curses.

THE HERD

I studied in the hedge school
and learned religions are a cod.
They're all the one.
Ask any fool.
Every lamb's a lamb of God.

From FREEHOLD

From THE LONELY HEART

Once in a seaside town with time to kill,
the windless winter-daylight ebbing chill,
the cafés shut till June, the shop blinds drawn,
only one pub yet open where a man
trundled his barrels off a dray with care,
and two men talking, small across the square,
I turned from broad street, down a red-brick row,
past prams in parlours and infrequent show
of thrusting bulbtips, till high steps and porch
and rigid statue signalised a church.
I climbed the granite past Saint Patrick's knees,
saw cross in stone, befingered, ringed with grease,
and water in a stoup with oily skin,
swung door on stall of booklets and went in
to the dim stained-glass cold interior
between low pews along a marble floor
to where the candles burned, still keeping pace
with ugly-coloured Stations of the Cross.
Two children tiptoed in and prayed awhile.
A shabby woman in a faded shawl
came hirpling past me then, and crumpled down,
crossing herself and mumbling monotone.

I stood and gazed across the altar rail
at the tall windows, cold and winter pale;
Christ and His Mother, Christ and Lazarus,
Christ watching Martha bustle round the house,
Christ crowned, with sceptre and a blessing hand.
I counted seven candles on the stand;
a box of matches of familiar brand
lay on a tray. It somehow seemed my right
to pay my penny and set up my light,
not to this coloured Christ nor to His Mother,
but single flame to sway with all the other
small earnest flames against the crowding gloom
which seemed that year descending on our time,
suppressed the fancy, smiled a cynic thought,
turned clicking heel on marble and went out.

Not this my fathers' faith: their walls are bare;
their comfort's all within, if anywhere.
I had gone there a vacant hour to pass,
to see the sculpture and admire the glass,
but left as I had come, a protestant,
and all unconscious of my yawning want;
too much intent on what to criticise
to give my heart the room to realise

that which endures the tides of time so long
cannot be always absolutely wrong;
not even with a friendly thought or human
for the two children and the praying woman.
The years since then have proved I should have stayed
and mercy might have touched me till I prayed.

For now I scorn no man's or child's belief
in any symbol that may succour grief
if we remember whence life first arose
and how within us yet that river flows;
and how the fabled shapes in dream's deep sea
still evidence our continuity
with being's seamless garment, web and thread.

O windblown grass upon the mounded dead,
O seed in crevice of the frost-split rock,
the power that fixed your root shall take us back,
though endlessly through aeons we are thrust
as luminous or unreflecting dust.

GAELIC MATTERS

From THE PASSING OF THE POETS

God help who follows his father's craft!
On Banba's fresh plain it happens
a father's trade is best no longer,
in the cool green fields of Ireland.

It seems that the poets' order
no longer, North or South,
may speak of their elders' work.
Let us turn to a different task,

not spinning the threads of wisdom
nor tracing our branching peoples
nor weaving a graceful verse
– nor talking of poetry.

The first who took to versing
might have turned to something else,
for he chose no lasting honour.
The arts reproach the scholar.

His teachers would better have shown him
horse training, or steering a ship,
or roping a plough to a bullock,
than manufacturing verse.

FEAR FLATHA Ó GNÍMH (EARLY 17TH CENT.)   41
TRANS. THOMAS KINSELLA

MY SON, FORSAKE YOUR ART

My son, forsake your art,
In that which was your fathers' own no part –
Though from the start she had borne pride of place,
Poetry now leads to disgrace.

Serve it not then, this leavings of a trade,
Nor by you be an Irish measure made,
Polished and perfect, whole in sound and sense –
Ape the new fashion, modish, cheap and dense.

Spin spineless verses of the commonplace,
Suffice it that they hold an even pace
And show not too nice taste within their span –
Preferment waits upon you if you can.

Give no man meed of censure nor just praise,
But if needs must your voice discreetly raise,
Not where there's only hatred to be earned,
Praising the Gael and for your labour spurned.

Break with them! Reckon not their histories
Nor chronicle them in men's memories,
Make it no study to enrich their fame,
Let all be named before an Irish name.

Thus you may purge your speech of bitterness,
Thus your addresses may command success –
What good repute has granted, do you hide,
Asperse their breeding, be their blood denied.

The good that has been, see you leave alone,
That which now goes for good dilate upon;
Polish the praises of a foreign rout,
Allies more likely as has come about.

The race of Miled and the Sons of Conn,
Who now maintains it, that their sway goes on?
A lying prophet in men's eyes to stand,
Proclaiming alien dynasts in the land!

The tribe of Lorc, proud Carthach's company,
Be these your strangers come from oversea,
Over Flann's ground girt with the smooth sea-ring,
Let none who bore their name bear it as king.

Conn of the Hundred Battles be forgot,
The son of Eochaidh hold you now as naught:
The stock of Conn, modest and generous,
Who had deserved a better fate from us.

Drive out of mind thought of their excellence,
Gerald's king-blood, our store of recompense,
Whom might no man for love of pelf condemn –
No poem ponder thou in praise of them.

For, since none now care,
For knowledge and the comely things that were,
And were not then like fencing in a plot,
The making of a poem shall profit not.

44   MATHGHAMLAIN Ó HIFEARNÁIN
        (EARLY 17TH CENT.)
        TRANS. MÁIRE CRUISE O'BRIEN

FOR THE FAMILY OF CÚCHONNACHT Ó DÁLAIGH

The high poets are gone
   and I mourn for the world's waning,
the sons of those learned masters
   emptied of sharp response.

I mourn for their fading books,
   reams of no earnest stupidity,
lost, unjustly abandoned,
   begotten by drinkers of wisdom.

After those poets, for whom art and knowledge were
      wealth,
   alas to have lived to see this fate befall us:
their books in corners greying into nothing
   and their sons without one syllable of their secret
      treasure.

A shrewish, barren, bony, nosy servant
refused me when my throat was parched in crisis.
May a phantom fly her starving over the sea,
the bloodless midget that wouldn't attend my thirst.

If I cursed her crime and herself, she'd learn a lesson.
The couple she serves would give me a cask on credit

but she growled at me in anger, and the beer nearby.
May the King of Glory not leave her long at her barrels.

A rusty little boiling with a musicless mouth,
she hurled me out with insult through the porch.
The Law requires I gloss over her pedigree
– but little the harm if she bore a cat to a ghost.

She's a club-footed slut and not a woman at all,
with the barrenest face you would meet on the
    open road,
and certain to be a fool to the end of the world.
May she drop her dung down stupidly into the
    porridge!

46   DÁIBHÍ Ó BRUADAIR (c. 1625–98)
    TRANS. THOMAS KINSELLA

THE BRIGHTEST OF THE BRIGHT

The Brightest of the Bright met me on my path
    so lonely;
  The Crystal of all Crystals was her flashing
     dark-blue eye;
Melodious more than music was her spoken language
    only;
  And glorious were her cheeks, of a brilliant
     crimson dye.

With ringlets above ringlets her hair in many a cluster
  Descended to the earth, and swept the dewy flowers;
Her bosom shone as bright as a mirror in its lustre;
  She seemed like some fair daughter of the Celestial
    Powers.

She chanted me a chant, a beautiful and grand hymn,
  Of him who should be shortly Éire's reigning King –
She prophesied the fall of the wretches who had
    banned him;
  And somewhat else she told me which I dare not sing.

Trembling with many fears I called on Holy Mary,
  As I drew nigh this Fair, to shield me from all harm,
When, wonderful to tell! she fled far to the Fairy
  Green mansions of Sliabh Luachra in terror and alarm.

O'er mountain, moor and marsh, by greenwood, lough
and hollow,
   I tracked her distant footsteps with a throbbing
heart;
Through many an hour and day did I follow on and
follow,
   Till I reached the magic palace reared of old by
Druid art.

There a wild and wizard band with mocking fiendish
laughter
   Pointed out me her I sought, who sat low beside
a clown;
And I felt as though I never could dream of Pleasure
after
   When I saw the maid so fallen whose charms
deserved a crown.

Then with burning speech and soul, I looked at her
and told her
   That to wed a churl like that was for her the shame
of shames
When a bridegroom such as I was longing to enfold her
   To a bosom that her beauty had enkindled into
flames.

But answer made she none; she wept with bitter
    weeping,
  Her tears ran down in rivers, but nothing could
      she say;
She gave me then a guide for my safe and better
    keeping, –
  The Brightest of the Bright, whom I met upon
      my way.

AOGÁN Ó RATHAILLE (*c.*1675–1729)
TRANS. JAMES CLARENCE MANGAN

From THE MIDNIGHT COURT

The Court considered the country's crisis,
And what do you think its main advice is –
That unless there's a spurt in procreation
We can bid goodbye to the Irish nation;
It's growing smaller year by year –
And don't pretend that's not your affair.
Between death and war and ruin and pillage
The land is like a deserted village;
Our best are banished, but you, you slob,
Have you ever hammered a single job?
What use are you to us, you cissy?
We have thousands of women who'd keep you busy,
With breasts like balloons or small as a bud,
Buxom of body and hot in the blood,
Virgins or whores – whatever's your taste –
At least don't let them go to waste;
It's enough to make us broken-hearted –
Legs galore – and none of them parted.
They're ready and willing for any endeavour –
But you can't expect them to wait forever.

THE OLD MAN'S TALE

The things I'm told, I could raise your hair
By recounting the times she's been stretched out bare,
On the flat of her back upon the ground
And the customers rushing from miles around.
From youth to grandad, all can speak
Of her adaptable technique –
In Ibrickane with big and small,
In Tirmaclane with one and all,
In Kilbrickane with thick and thin,
in Clare, in Ennis, and in Quin,
In Cratlee and Tradree where they're tough
She never seemed to have enough!
But I'd still have allowed her a second chance
And blamed it on youthful extravagance
Were it not that I saw with my own two eyes
On the roadway – naked to the skies –
Herself and a lout from the Durrus bogs
Going hammer and tongs like a couple of dogs.

BRIAN MERRIMAN (1747–1805)   51
TRANS. DAVID MARCUS

'I AM RAIFTEIRÍ, THE POET'

I am Raifteirí, the poet, full of courage and love,
my eyes without light, in calmness serene,
taking my way by the light of my heart
feeble and tired to the end of the road:
look at me now, my face toward Balla,
playing my music to empty pockets!

DEIRDRE'S LAMENT FOR THE SONS OF USNACH
(*From the Irish*)

The lions of the hill are gone,
And I am left alone – alone –
Dig the grave both wide and deep,
For I am sick, and fain would sleep!

The falcons of the wood are flown,
And I am left alone – alone –
Dig the grave both deep and wide,
And let us slumber side by side.

The dragons of the rock are sleeping,
Sleep that wakes not for our weeping:
Dig the grave and make it ready;
Lay me on my true Love's body.

Lay their spears and bucklers bright
By the warriors' sides aright;
Many a day the Three before me
On their linkèd bucklers bore me.

Lay upon the low grave floor,
'Neath each head, the blue claymore;
Many a time the noble Three
Redden'd those blue blades for me.

Lay the collars, as is meet,
Of their greyhounds at their feet;
Many a time for me have they
Brought the tall red deer to bay.

Oh! to hear my true Love singing,
Sweet as sound of trumpets ringing:
Like the sway of ocean swelling
Roll'd his deep voice round our dwelling.

Oh! to hear the echoes pealing
Round our green and fairy sheeling,
When the Three, with soaring chorus,
Pass'd the silent skylark o'er us.

Echo now, sleep, morn and even –
Lark alone enchant the heaven! –
Ardan's lips are scant of breath, –
Neesa's tongue is cold in death.

Stag, exult on glen and mountain –
Salmon, leap from loch to fountain –
Heron, in the free air warm ye –
Usnach's Sons no more will harm ye!

Erin's stay no more you are,
Rulers of the ridge of war;
Never more 'twill be your fate
To keep the beam of battle straight.

Woe is me! by fraud and wrong –
Traitors false and tyrants strong –
Fell Clan Usnach, bought and sold,
For Barach's feast and Conor's gold!

Woe to Eman, roof and wall! –
Woe to Red Branch, hearth and hall! –
Tenfold woe and black dishonour
To the false and foul Clan Conor!

Dig the grave both wide and deep,
Sick I am, and fain would sleep!
Dig the grave and make it ready,
Lay me on my true Love's body.

THE FAIRIES

Up the airy mountain,
  Down the rushy glen,
We daren't go a-hunting
  For fear of little men;
Wee folk, good folk,
  Trooping all together;
Green jacket, red cap,
  And white owl's feather!

Down along the rocky shore
  Some make their home,
They live on crispy pancakes,
  Of yellow tide-foam;
Some in the reeds
  Of the bleak mountain lake,
With frogs for their watch-dogs,
  All night awake.

High on the hill-top
  The old King sits;
He is now so old and gray
  He's nigh lost his wits.
With a bridge of white mist
  Columbkill he crosses,
On his stately journeys
  From Sleeveleague to Rosses;

Or going up with music
   On cold starry nights,
To sup with the Queen
   Of the gay Northern Lights.

They stole little Bridget
   For seven years long;
When she came down again
   Her friends were all gone.
They took her lightly back,
   Between the night and morrow,
They thought that she was fast asleep,
   But she was dead with sorrow.
They have kept her ever since
   Deep within the lake,
On a bed of flag-leaves,
   Watching till she wake.

By the craggy hillside
   Through the mosses bare,
They have planted thorn-trees
   For pleasure here and there.
If any man so daring
   As dig them up in spite,
He shall find their sharpest thorns
   In his bed at night.

Up the airy mountain,
    Down the rushy glen,
We daren't go a-hunting
    For fear of little men;
Wee folk, good folk,
    Trooping all together;
Green jacket, red cap,
    And white owl's feather!

CUCHULAIN'S FIGHT WITH THE SEA

A man came slowly from the setting sun,
To Emer, raddling raiment in her dun,
And said, 'I am that swineherd whom you bid
Go watch the road between the wood and tide,
But now I have no need to watch it more.'

Then Emer cast the web upon the floor,
And raising arms all raddled with the dye,
Parted her lips with a loud sudden cry.

That swineherd stared upon her face and said,
'No man alive, no man among the dead,
Has won the gold his cars of battle bring.'

'But if your master comes home triumphing
Why must you blench and shake from foot to crown?'

Thereon he shook the more and cast him down
Upon the web-heaped floor, and cried his word:
'With him is one sweet-throated like a bird.'

'You dare me to my face,' and thereupon
She smote with raddled fist, and where her son

Herded the cattle came with stumbling feet,
And cried with angry voice, 'It is not meet
To idle life away, a common herd.'

'I have long waited, mother, for that word:
But wherefore now?'
                          'There is a man to die;
You have the heaviest arm under the sky.'

'Whether under its daylight or its stars
My father stands amid his battle-cars.'

'But you have grown to be the taller man.'

'Yet somewhere under starlight or the sun
My father stands.'
                          'Aged, worn out with wars
On foot, on horseback or in battle-cars.'

'I only ask what way my journey lies,
For He who made you bitter made you wise.'

'The Red Branch camp in a great company
Between wood's rim and the horses of the sea.
Go there, and light a camp-fire at wood's rim;
But tell your name and lineage to him
Whose blade compels, and wait till they have found
Some feasting man that the same oath has bound.'

Among those feasting men Cuchulain dwelt,
And his young sweetheart close beside him knelt,
Stared on the mournful wonder of his eyes,
Even as Spring upon the ancient skies,
And pondered on the glory of his days;
And all around the harp-string told his praise,
And Conchubar, the Red Branch king of kings,
With his own fingers touched the brazen strings.

At last Cuchulain spake, 'Some man has made
His evening fire amid the leafy shade.
I have often heard him singing to and fro,
I have often heard the sweet sound of his bow.
Seek out what man he is.'

                One went and came.
'He bade me let all know he gives his name
At the sword-point, and waits till we have found
Some feasting man that the same oath has bound.'

Cuchulain cried, 'I am the only man
Of all this host so bound from childhood on.'

After short fighting in the leafy shade,
He spake to the young man, 'Is there no maid
Who loves you, no white arms to wrap you round,
Or do you long for the dim sleepy ground,
That you have come and dared me to my face?'

'The dooms of men are in God's hidden place.'

'Your head a while seemed like a woman's head
That I loved once.'
                    Again the fighting sped,
But now the war-rage in Cuchulain woke,
And through that new blade's guard the old
        blade broke,
And pierced him.
                'Speak before your breath is done.'

'Cuchulain I, mighty Cuchulain's son.'

'I put you from your pain. I can no more.'

While day its burden on to evening bore,
With head bowed on his knees Cuchulain stayed;
Then Conchubar sent that sweet-throated maid,
And she, to win him, his grey hair caressed;
In vain her arms, in vain her soft white breast.
Then Conchubar, the subtlest of all men,
Ranking his Druids round him ten by ten,
Spake thus: 'Cuchulain will dwell there and brood
For three days more in dreadful quietude,
And then arise, and raving slay us all.
Chaunt in his ear delusions magical,
That he may fight the horses of the sea.'

The Druids took them to their mystery,
And chaunted for three days.

                    Cuchulain stirred,
Stared on the horses of the sea, and heard
The cars of battle and his own name cried;
And fought with the invulnerable tide.

CLAUSTROPHOBIA

Next to the wine
Stand a candle and terror,
The statue of my Lord
Bereft of its power;
What's left of the night
Is massing in the yard,
Night's empire
Is outside the window;
If my candle fails
Despite my efforts
The night will leap
Right into my lungs,
My mind will collapse
And terror be made for me,
Taken over by night,
I'll be darkness alive:
    But if my candle lasts
    Just this one night
    I'll be a republic of light
    Until dawn.

SEÁN Ó RÍORDÁIN (1917–77)
TRANS. PATRICK CROTTY

MIRACULOUS GRASS

There you were in your purple vestments
half-way through the Mass, an ordained priest
under your linen alb and chasuble and stole:
and when you saw my face in the crowd
for Holy Communion
the consecrated host fell from your fingers.

I felt shame, I never
mentioned it once,
my lips were sealed.
But still it lurked in my heart
like a thorn under mud, and it
worked itself in so deep and sheer
it nearly killed me.

Next thing then, I was laid up in bed.
Consultants came in their hundreds,
doctors and brothers and priests,
but I baffled them all: I was
incurable, they left me for dead.

So out you go, men,
out with the spades and scythes,
the hooks and shovels and hoes.
Tackle the rubble,

cut back the bushes, clear off the rubbish,
the sappy growth, the whole straggle and mess
that infests my green unfortunate field.

And there where the sacred wafer fell
you will discover
in the middle of the shooting weeds
a clump of miraculous grass.

The priest will have to come then
with his delicate fingers, and lift the host
and bring it to me and put it on my tongue.
Where it will melt, and I will rise in the bed
as fit and well as the youngster I used to be.

POLITICAL
MATTERS

From THE FLIGHT OF THE EARLS, 1607

All Ireland's now one vessel's company,
And riding west by cliffs of Beare to sea.
Upon the snowy foam of the ebbing tide
Away in one frail bark goes all our pride.
Now stolen is the soul from Éire's breast,
And all her coasts and islands mourn oppressed.
The great twin eagles of the flock of Conn
In perilous flight are in one vessel gone.
For they whose pinions shaded Ulster's plain
In their high bark have gone nor come again;
Two last and yet most royal birds of all
Fly westward to the sea beyond recall . . .
Rory our darling, and our most gracious Hugh!
And tho' we named no names beyond the two,
Yet in this sailing have we lost a host
Of men that fainting Ireland needed most . . .

Now let the hearts of all rejoice again,
For our great Earls have safely come to Spain;
And yet their going o'er the sea must fill
With bitter wailing Éire's every hill.
Comparing their good fortune, being away,
With their sad impotence if they should stay,
Let Uisneach's land lament and yet rejoice,
And gloom and glory mingle now their voice.

And yet to know that they are gone from me,
And sail with good success beyond the sea,
Has left me lying in affliction sore.
Alas, for them, for me, for evermore!

FEARGHAL ÓG MacWARD (1550–1615)
TRANS. EARL OF LONGFORD

THE CROPPY BOY

It was early, early in the spring,
The birds did whistle and sweetly sing,
Changing their notes from tree to tree
And the song they sang was 'Old Ireland Free'.

It was early, early in the night,
The Yeoman cavalry gave me a fright,
The Yeoman cavalry was my downfall
And I was taken by Lord Cornwall.

It was in the coach house that I was laid
And in the parlour that I was tried.
My sentence passed and my courage low
As to Duncannon I was forced to go.

As I was going up Wexford Street
My own first cousin I chanced to meet.
My own first cousin did me betray
And for one bare guinea swore my life away.

As I was passing my father's door
My brother William stood in the door,
My aged father stood there before
And my own dear mother her hair she tore.

As I was going up Wexford Hill
Oh who would blame me to cry my fill?
I looked behind and I looked before
And my own dear mother I shall ne'er see more.

As I was standing on the scaffold high
My own dear father was standing nigh.
My own dear father did me deny
And the name he gave me was 'The Croppy Boy'.

It was in Duncannon this young man died
And in Duncannon his body was laid.
Now all good people that do pass by
O spare a tear for 'The Croppy Boy'.

THE SHAN VAN VOCHT

Oh! the French are on the sea,
    Says the *Shan Van vocht*;
The French are on the sea,
    Says the *Shan Van vocht*;
Oh! the French are in the bay,
They'll be here without delay,
And the Orange will decay,
    Says the *Shan Van vocht*.

CHORUS
Oh! the French are in the bay,
They'll be here by break of day,
And the Orange will decay,
    Says the *Shan Van vocht*.

And where will they have their camp?
    Says the *Shan Van vocht*;
Where will they have their camp?
    Says the *Shan Van vocht*;
On the Currach of Kildare,
The boys they will be there
With their pikes in good repair,
    Says the *Shan Van vocht*.

To the Currach of Kildare
The boys they will repair,
And Lord Edward will be there,
    Says the *Shan Van vocht*.

Then what will the yeomen do?
    Says the *Shan Van vocht*;
What *will* the yeomen do?
    Says the *Shan Van vocht*;
What *should* the yeomen do,
But throw off the red and blue,
And swear that they'll be true
    To the *Shan Van vocht*.

What *should* the yeomen do
But throw off the red and blue,
And swear that they'll be true
    To the *Shan Van vocht*.

And what colour will they wear?
    Says the *Shan Van vocht*;
What colour will they wear?
    Says the *Shan Van vocht*;
What colour should be seen
Where our fathers' homes have been,
But their own immortal Green?
    Says the *Shan Van vocht*.

What colour should be seen
Where our fathers' homes have been,
But their own immortal Green?
   Says the *Shan Van vocht*.

And will Ireland then be free?
   Says the *Shan Van vocht*;
Will Ireland then be free?
   Says the *Shan Van vocht*;
Yes! Ireland SHALL be free,
From the centre to the sea;
Then hurra for Liberty!
   Says the *Shan Van vocht*.

Yes! Ireland SHALL be free,
From the centre to the sea;
Then hurra for Liberty!
   Says the *Shan Van vocht*.

ANON. (19TH CENT.)   75

THE ORANGE LILY

My dear Orange brothers, have you heard of the news,
How the treacherous Frenchmen our gulls to amuse,
The troops that last April they promised to send,
At length at Killala they ventured to land.
   Good Croppies, but don't be too bold now,
   Lest you should be all stow'd in the hold now,
   Then to Bot'ny you'd trudge, I am told now,
     And a sweet orange lily for me.

But now that they're landed they find their mistake,
For in place of the Croppies they meet the brave Lake;
He soon will convince them that our orange and blue
Can ne'er be subdued by their plundering crew.
   Good Croppies, then don't, etc.

That false traitor Emmet, more ungrateful than hell,
With McNevin and Arthur, though fast in their cell;
What they formerly swore they have dar'd to deny,
And the Secret Committee have charg'd with a lie!
   Good Croppies, then don't, etc.

But as, by this falsehood, it is clear they intend
To induce us poor peasants the French to befriend;
We shall soon, I hope, see them high dangling in air,
'Twould be murd'ring the loyal such miscreants to spare.
   Good Croppies, then don't, etc.

On the trees at the camp Crop Lawless intended,
To hang up all those who their country defended;
As the scene is reversed, a good joke it will be,
In the place of dear Camden to put up those three.
    Good Croppies then don't, etc.

Judgment being entered on that bloody Bond,
Execution should follow, the people contend;
Why stay it, say they, when engagements they've
      broken?
The Direct'ry deny ev'ry word they had spoken.
    Good Croppies, then don't, etc.

Then gird on your sabres, my brave Orangemen all,
For the Croppies are down, and the Frenchmen
      shall fall;
Let each lodge sally forth, from one to nine hundred.
Those freebooters ere long with the dead shall be
      number'd.
    Good Croppies, then don't, etc.

KATHALEEN NY-HOULAHAN

Long they pine in weary woe, the nobles of our land,
Long they wander to and fro, proscribed, alas! and
    banned;
Feastless, houseless, altarless, they bear the exile's
    brand,
  But their hope is in the coming-to of Kathaleen
    Ny-Houlahan!

Think her not a ghastly hag, too hideous to be seen,
Call her not unseemly names, our matchless
    Kathaleen;
Young she is, and fair she is, and would be crowned a
    queen,
  Were the king's son at home here with Kathaleen
    Ny-Houlahan!

Sweet and mild would look her face, O, none so sweet
    and mild,
Could she crush the foes by whom her beauty is reviled;
Woollen plaids would grace herself and robes of silk
    her child,
  If the king's son were living here with Kathaleen
    Ny-Houlahan!

Sore disgrace it is to see the Arbitress of thrones,
Vassal to a *Saxoneen* of cold and sapless bones!
Bitter anguish wrings our souls – with heavy sighs
    and groans
  We wait the Young Deliverer of Kathaleen
      Ny-Houlahan!

Let us pray to Him who holds Life's issues in His
    hands –
Him who formed the mighty globe, with all its
    thousand lands;
Girding them with seas and mountains, rivers deep,
    and strands,
  To cast a look of pity upon Kathaleen Ny-Houlahan!

He, who over sands and waves led Israël along –
He, who fed, with heavenly bread, that chosen tribe
    and throng –
He, who stood by Moses, when his foes were fierce
    and strong –
  May He show forth His might in saving Kathaleen
      Ny-Houlahan.

LAMENT FOR THE DEATH OF EOGHAN RUADH O'NEILL

COMMONLY CALLED OWEN ROE O'NEIL

'Did they dare, did they dare, to slay Owen Roe O'Neil?'
'Yes, they slew with poison him they feared to meet
with steel.'
'May God wither up their hearts! May their blood
cease to flow!
May they walk in living death, who poisoned
Owen Roe!

'Though it break my heart to hear, say again the bitter
words.'
'From Derry, against Cromwell, he marched to
measure swords;
But the weapon of the Saxon met him on his way,
And he died at Cloc Uactair, upon Saint Leonard's Day.'

'Wail, wail ye for the Mighty One! Wail, wail ye for
the Dead!
Quench the hearth, and hold the breath – with ashes
strew the head!
How tenderly we loved him! How deeply we deplore!
Holy Saviour! but to think we shall never see him more!

'Sagest in the council was he, kindest in the hall:
Sure we never won a battle – 'twas Owen won them all.
Had he lived, had he lived, our dear country had
    been free;
But he's dead, but he's dead, and 'tis slaves we'll ever be.

'O'Farrell and Clanrickarde, Preston and Red Hugh,
Audley and MacMahon, ye are valiant, wise, and true;
But what – what are ye all to our darling who is gone?
The rudder of our ship was he – our castle's
    corner-stone!

'Wail, wail him through the island! Weep, weep for
    our pride!
Would that on the battlefield our gallant chief had died!
Weep the victor of Beinn Burb – weep him, young men
    and old!
Weep for him, ye women – your Beautiful lies cold!

'We thought you would not die – we were sure you
    would not go,
And leave us in our utmost need to Cromwell's cruel
    blow –

Sheep without a shepherd, when the snow shuts out
     the sky –
Oh! why did you leave us, Owen? why did you die?

'Soft as woman's was your voice, O'Neil! bright was
     your eye!
Oh! why did you leave us, Owen? why did you die?
Your troubles are all over – you're at rest with God
     on high;
But we're slaves, and we're orphans, Owen! – why did
     you die?'

A NATION ONCE AGAIN

When boyhood's fire was in my blood,
    I read of ancient freemen,
For Greece and Rome who bravely stood,
    Three Hundred men and Three men.
And then I prayed I yet might see
    Our fetters rent in twain,
And Ireland, long a province, be
    A Nation once again.

And, from that time, through wildest woe,
    That hope has shone, a far light;
Nor could love's brightest summer glow
    Outshine that solemn starlight:
It seemed to watch above my head
    In forum, field, and fane;
Its angel voice sang round my bed,
    'A Nation once again'.

It whispered, too, that 'freedom's ark
    And service high and holy,
Would be profaned by feelings dark,
    And passions vain or lowly;
For freedom comes from God's right hand,
    And needs a godly train;
And righteous men must make our land
    A Nation once again.'

So, as I grew from boy to man,
  I bent me to that bidding –
My spirit of each selfish plan
  And cruel passion ridding;
For, thus I hoped some day to aid –
  Oh! can such hope be vain?
When my dear country shall be made
  A Nation once again.

THE WIND THAT SHAKES THE BARLEY

I sat within a valley green
I sat me with my true love
My sad heart strove to choose between
The old love and the new love
The old for her, the new that made
Me think on Ireland dearly
While soft the wind blew down the glade
And shook the golden barley

'Twas hard the woeful words to frame
To break the ties that bound us
But harder still to bear the shame
Of foreign chains around us
And so I said, 'The mountain glen
I'll seek at morning early
And join the bold United Men
While soft winds shake the barley'

While sad I kissed away her tears
My fond arms 'round her flinging
The foeman's shot burst on our ears
From out the wildwood ringing
A bullet pierced my true love's side
In life's young spring so early
And on my breast in blood she died
While soft winds shook the barley

I bore her to some mountain stream
And many's the summer blossom
I placed with branches soft and green
About her gore-stained bosom
I wept and kissed her clay-cold corpse
Then rushed o'er vale and valley
My vengeance on the foe to wreak
While soft winds shook the barley

But blood for blood without remorse
I've taken at Oulart Hollow
And laid my true love's clay-cold corpse
Where I full soon may follow
As 'round her grave I wander drear
Noon, night and morning early
With breaking heart when e'er I hear
The wind that shakes the barley.

SEPTEMBER 1913

What need you, being come to sense,
But fumble in a greasy till
And add the halfpence to the pence
And prayer to shivering prayer, until
You have dried the marrow from the bone?
For men were born to pray and save:
Romantic Ireland's dead and gone,
It's with O'Leary in the grave.

Yet they were of a different kind,
The names that stilled your childish play,
They have gone about the world like wind,
But little time had they to pray
For whom the hangman's rope was spun,
And what, God help us, could they save?
Romantic Ireland's dead and gone,
It's with O'Leary in the grave.

Was it for this the wild geese spread
The grey wing upon every tide;
For this that all that blood was shed,
For this Edward Fitzgerald died,
And Robert Emmet and Wolfe Tone,
All that delirium of the brave?
Romantic Ireland's dead and gone,
It's with O'Leary in the grave.

Yet could we turn the years again,
And call those exiles as they were
In all their loneliness and pain,
You'd cry, 'Some woman's yellow hair
Has maddened every mother's son':
They weighed so lightly what they gave.
But let them be, they're dead and gone,
They're with O'Leary in the grave.

THE WILD SWANS AT COOLE

The trees are in their autumn beauty,
The woodland paths are dry,
Under the October twilight the water
Mirrors a still sky;
Upon the brimming water among the stones
Are nine-and-fifty swans.

The nineteenth autumn has come upon me
Since I first made my count;
I saw, before I had well finished,
All suddenly mount
And scatter wheeling in great broken rings
Upon their clamorous wings.

I have looked upon those brilliant creatures,
And now my heart is sore.
All's changed since I, hearing at twilight,
The first time on this shore,
The bell-beat of their wings above my head,
Trod with a lighter tread.

Unwearied still, lover by lover,
They paddle in the cold
Companionable streams or climb the air;
Their hearts have not grown old;

Passion or conquest, wander where they will,
Attend upon them still.

But now they drift on the still water,
Mysterious, beautiful;
Among what rushes will they build,
By what lake's edge or pool
Delight men's eyes when I awake some day
To find they have flown away?

REQUIEM FOR THE CROPPIES

The pockets of our greatcoats full of barley –
No kitchens on the run, no striking camp –
We moved quick and sudden in our own country
The priest lay behind ditches with the tramp.
A people, hardly marching – on the hike –
We found new tactics happening each day:
We'd cut through reins and rider with the pike
And stampede cattle into infantry,
Then retreat through hedges where cavalry must
    be thrown.
Until, on Vinegar Hill, the fatal conclave.
Terraced thousands died, shaking scythes at cannon.
The hillside blushed, soaked in our broken wave.
They buried us without shroud or coffin
And in August the barley grew up out of the grave.

SEAMUS HEANEY (1939–)

PUNISHMENT

I can feel the tug
of the halter at the nape
of her neck, the wind
on her naked front.

It blows her nipples
to amber beads,
it shakes the frail rigging
of her ribs.

I can see her drowned
body in the bog,
the weighing stone,
the floating rods and boughs.

Under which at first
she was a barked sapling
that is dug up
oak-bone, brain-firkin:

her shaved head
like a stubble of black corn,
her blindfold a soiled bandage,
her noose a ring

to store
the memories of love.
Little adulteress,
before they punished you

you were flaxen-haired,
undernourished, and your
tar-black face was beautiful.
My poor scapegoat,

I almost love you
but would have cast, I know,
the stones of silence.
I am the artful voyeur

of your brain's exposed
and darkened combs,
your muscles' webbing
and all your numbered bones:

I who have stood dumb
when your betraying sisters,
cauled in tar,
wept by the railings,

who would connive
in civilized outrage
yet understand the exact
and tribal, intimate revenge.

From WHATEVER YOU SAY SAY NOTHING

I

I'm writing this just after an encounter
With an English journalist in search of 'views
On the Irish thing'. I'm back in winter
Quarters where bad news is no longer news,

Where media-men and stringers sniff and point,
Where zoom lenses, recorders and coiled leads
Litter the hotels. The times are out of joint
But I incline as much to rosary beads

As to the jottings and analyses
Of politicians and newspapermen
Who've scribbled down the long campaign from gas
And protest to gelignite and Sten,

Who proved upon their pulses 'escalate',
'Backlash' and 'crack down', 'the provisional wing',
'Polarization' and 'long-standing hate'.
Yet I live here, I live here too, I sing,

Expertly civil-tongued with civil neighbours
On the high wires of first wireless reports,
Sucking the fake taste, the stony flavours
Of those sanctioned, old, elaborate retorts:

'Oh, it's disgraceful, surely, I agree.'
'Where's it going to end?' 'It's getting worse.'
'They're murderers.' 'Internment, understandably...'
The 'voice of sanity' is getting hoarse.

III
'Religion's never mentioned here,' of course.
'You know them by their eyes,' and hold your tongue.
'One side's as bad as the other,' never worse.
Christ, it's near time that some small leak was sprung

In the great dykes the Dutchman made
To dam the dangerous tide that followed Seamus.
Yet for all this art and sedentary trade
I am incapable. The famous

Northern reticence, the tight gag of place
And times: yes, yes. Of the 'wee six' I sing
Where to be saved you only must save face
And whatever you say, you say nothing.

Smoke-signals are loud-mouthed compared with us:
Manoeuvrings to find out name and school,
Subtle discrimination by addresses
With hardly an exception to the rule

That Norman, Ken and Sidney signalled Prod
And Seamus (call me Sean) was sure-fire Pape.
O land of password, handgrip, wink and nod,
Of open minds as open as a trap,

Where tongues lie coiled, as under flames lie wicks,
Where half of us, as in a wooden horse,
Were cabin'd and confined like wily Greeks,
Besieged within the siege, whispering morse.

IV

This morning from a dewy motorway
I saw the new camp for the internees:
A bomb had left a crater of fresh clay
In the roadside, and over in the trees

Machine-gun posts defined a real stockade.
There was that white mist you get on a low ground
And it was déjà-vu, some film made
Of Stalag 17, a bad dream with no sound.

Is there a life before death? That's chalked up
In Ballymurphy. Competence with pain,
Coherent miseries, a bite and sup:
We hug our little destiny again.

SEAMUS HEANEY (1939–)

From THE CURE AT TROY

CHORUS
Human beings suffer.
They torture one another.
They get hurt and get hard.
No poem or play or song
Can fully right a wrong
Inflicted and endured.

History says, Don't hope
On this side of the grave,
But then, once in a lifetime
The longed-for tidal wave
Of justice can rise up
And hope and history rhyme.

So hope for a great sea-change
On the far side of revenge.
Believe that a farther shore
Is reachable from here.
Believe in miracles
And cures and healing wells.

Call miracle self-healing,
The utter self-revealing
Double-take of feeling.
If there's fire on the mountain
And lightning and storm
And a god speaks from the sky

That means someone is hearing
The outcry and the birth-cry
Of new life at its term.
It means once in a lifetime
That justice can rise up
And hope and history rhyme.

A DISUSED SHED IN CO. WEXFORD

Let them not forget us, the weak souls among the asphodels.
GEORGE SEFERIS, *Mythistorema*, tr. Keeley and Sherrard

for J.G. Farrell

Even now there are places where a thought
    might grow –
Peruvian mines, worked out and abandoned
To a slow clock of condensation,
An echo trapped for ever, and a flutter
Of wild-flowers in the lift-shaft,
Indian compounds where the wind dances
And a door bangs with diminished confidence,
Lime crevices behind rippling rain-barrels,
Dog corners for bone burials;
And in a disused shed in Co. Wexford,

Deep in the grounds of a burnt-out hotel,
Among the bathtubs and the washbasins
A thousand mushrooms crowd to a keyhole.
This is the one star in their firmament
Or frames a star within a star.
What should they do there but desire?
So many days beyond the rhododendrons
With the world waltzing in its bowl of cloud,
They have learnt patience and silence
Listening to the rooks querulous in the high wood.

They have been waiting for us in a foetor
Of vegetable sweat since civil war days,
Since the gravel-crunching, interminable departure
Of the expropriated mycologist.
He never came back, and light since then
Is a keyhole rusting gently after rain.
Spiders have spun, flies dusted to mildew
And once a day, perhaps, they have heard something –
A trickle of masonry, a shout from the blue
Or a lorry changing gear at the end of the lane.

There have been deaths, the pale flesh flaking
Into the earth that nourished it;
And nightmares, born of these and the grim
Dominion of stale air and rank moisture.
Those nearest the door grow strong –
'Elbow room! Elbow room!'
The rest, dim in a twilight of crumbling
Utensils and broken pitchers, groaning
For their deliverance, have been so long
Expectant that there is left only the posture.

A half century, without visitors, in the dark –
Poor preparation for the cracking lock
And creak of hinges. Magi, moonmen,
Powdery prisoners of the old regime,
Web-throated, stalked like triffids, racked by drought
And insomnia, only the ghost of a scream
At the flash-bulb firing-squad we wake them with
Shows there is life yet in their feverish forms.
Grown beyond nature now, soft food for worms,
They lift frail heads in gravity and good faith.

They are begging us, you see, in their wordless way,
To do something, to speak on their behalf
Or at least not to close the door again.
Lost people of Treblinka and Pompeii!
'Save us, save us,' they seem to say,
'Let the god not abandon us
Who have come so far in darkness and in pain.
We too had our lives to live.
You with your light meter and relaxed itinerary,
Let not our naive labours have been in vain!'

DEATHS AND ENGINES

We came down above the houses
In a stiff curve, and
At the edge of Paris airport
Saw an empty tunnel
– The back half of a plane, black
On the snow, nobody near it,
Tubular, burnt-out and frozen.

When we faced again
The snow-white runways in the dark
No sound came over
The loudspeakers, except the sighs
Of the lonely pilot.

The cold of metal wings is contagious:
Soon you will need wings of your own,
Cornered in the angle where
Time and life like a knife and fork
Cross, and the lifeline in your palm
Breaks, and the curve of an aeroplane's track
Meets the straight skyline.

The images of relief:
Hospital pyjamas, screens round a bed
A man with a bloody face

Sitting up in bed, conversing cheerfully
Through cut lips:
These will fail you some time.

You will find yourself alone
Accelerating down a blind
Alley, too late to stop
And know how light your death is;
You will be scattered like wreckage,
The pieces every one a different shape
Will spin and lodge in the hearts
Of all who love you.

LUNCH WITH PANCHO VILLA

I

'Is it really a revolution, though?'
I reached across the wicker table
With another $10,000 question.
My celebrated pamphleteer,
Co-author of such volumes
As *Blood on the Rose*,
The Dream and the Drums,
And *How It Happened Here*,
Would pour some untroubled Muscatel
And settle back in his cane chair.

'Look, son. Just look around you.
People are getting themselves killed
Left, right and centre
While you do what? Write rondeaux?
There's more to living in this country
Than stars and horses, pigs and trees,
Not that you'd guess it from your poems.
Do you never listen to the news?
You want to get down to something true,
Something a little nearer home.'

I called again later that afternoon,
A quiet suburban street.

'You want to stand back a little
When the world's at your feet.'
I'd have liked to have heard some more
Of his famous revolution.
I rang the bell, and knocked hard
On what I remembered as his front door,
That opened then, as such doors do,
Directly on to a back yard.

II
Not any back yard, I'm bound to say,
And not a thousand miles away
From here. No one's taken in, I'm sure,
By such a mild invention.
But where (I wonder myself) do I stand,
In relation to a table and chair,
The quince-tree I forgot to mention,
That suburban street, the door, the yard –
All made up as I went along
As things that people live among.

And such a person as lived there!
My celebrated pamphleteer!
Of course, I gave it all away
With those preposterous titles.
The Bloody Rose? The Dream and the Drums?
The three-day-wonder of the flowering plum!

Or was I desperately wishing
To have been their other co-author.
Or, at least, to own a first edition
Of *The Boot Boys and Other Battles*?

'When are you going to tell the truth?'
For there's no such book, so far as I know,
As *How It Happened Here*,
Though there may be. There may.
What should I say to this callow youth
Who learned to write last winter –
One of those correspondence courses –
And who's coming to lunch today?
He'll be rambling on, no doubt,
About pigs and trees, stars and horses.

ANSEO

When the Master was calling the roll
At the primary school in Collegelands,
You were meant to call back *Anseo*
And raise your hand
As your name occurred.
Anseo, meaning here, here and now,
All present and correct,
Was the first word of Irish I spoke.
The last name on the ledger
Belonged to Joseph Mary Plunkett Ward
And was followed, as often as not,
By silence, knowing looks,
A nod and a wink, the Master's droll
'And where's our little Ward-of-court?'

I remember the first time he came back
The Master had sent him out
Along the hedges
To weigh up for himself and cut
A stick with which he would be beaten.
After a while, nothing was spoken;
He would arrive as a matter of course
With an ash-plant, a salley-rod.
Or, finally, the hazel-wand
He had whittled down to a whip-lash,

Its twist of red and yellow lacquers
Sanded and polished,
And altogether so delicately wrought
That he had engraved his initials on it.

I last met Joseph Mary Plunkett Ward
In a pub just over the Irish border.
He was living in the open,
In a secret camp
On the other side of the mountain.
He was fighting for Ireland,
Making things happen.
And he told me, Joe Ward,
Of how he had risen through the ranks
To Quartermaster, Commandant:
How every morning at parade
His volunteers would call back *Anseo*
And raise their hands
As their names occurred.

CUBA

My eldest sister arrived home that morning
In her white muslin evening dress.
'Who the hell do you think you are,
Running out to dances in next to nothing?
As though we hadn't enough bother
With the world at war, if not at an end.'
My father was pounding the breakfast-table.

'Those Yankees were touch and go as it was –
If you'd heard Patton in Armagh –
But this Kennedy's nearly an Irishman
So he's not much better than ourselves.
And him with only to say the word.
If you've got anything on your mind
Maybe you should make your peace with God.'

I could hear May from beyond the curtain.
'Bless me, Father, for I have sinned.
I told a lie once, I was disobedient once.
And, Father, a boy touched me once.'
'Tell me, child. Was this touch immodest?
Did he touch your breast, for example?'
'He brushed against me, Father. Very gently.'

PROGRESS

They say that for years Belfast was backwards
and it's great now to see some progress.
So I guess we can look forward to taking boxes
from the earth. I guess that ambulances
will leave the dying back amidst the rubble
to be explosively healed. Given time,
one hundred thousand particles of glass
will create impossible patterns in the air
before coalescing into the clarity
of a window. Through which, a reassembled head
will look out and admire the shy young man
taking his bomb from the building and driving home.

ALAN GILLIS (1973–)   111

SECONDS OUT

After Humpty Dumpty fell apart
they said they would reconstitute him
in the Tat factory
iron out the folds in his carapace
rebuild him with sellotape and cowgum
three square meals a day
and some confrontation therapy

It would be hard they said
a stiff course for an egg
— an egg who suspected he'd be better off
robbing mail trains
or turning tricks on the canal bank —
a stiff course for an egg
but they would make a man of him

As in the end they did
a man of weights and measures
stripping five hundred crocus flowers
to procure an ounce of saffron

PLACE MATTERS

RACE MATTERS

HOLYHEAD. SEPT. 25TH, 1727

Lo here I sit at holy head
With muddy ale and mouldy bread
All Christian vittals stink of fish
I'm where my enemyes would wish
Convict of lyes is every sign,
The Inn has not one drop of wine
I'm fasnd both by wind and tide
I see the ship at anchor ride
The Captain swears the sea's too rough
He has not passengers enough.
And thus the Dean is forc't to stay
Till others come to help the pay.
In Dublin they'll be glad to see
A packet though it brings in me.
They cannot say the winds are cross
Your Politicians at a loss
For want of matter swears and fretts,
Are forced to read the old gazettes.
I never was in hast before
To reach that slavish hateful shore
Before, I always found the wind
To me was most malicious kind
But now, the danger of a friend
On whom my fears and hopes depend
Absent from whom all Clymes are curst

With whom I'm happy in the worst
With rage impatient makes me wait
A passenger to the land I hate.
Else, rather on this bleaky shore
Where loudest winds incessant roar
Where neither herb nor tree will thrive,
Where nature hardly seems alive,
I'd go in freedom to my grave,
Than Rule yon Isle and be a Slave.

From THE DESERTED VILLAGE

Sweet smiling village, loveliest of the lawn,
Thy sports are fled, and all thy charms withdrawn;
Amidst thy bowers the tyrant's hand is seen,
And desolation saddens all thy green:
One only master grasps the whole domain,
And half a tillage stints thy smiling plain:
No more thy glassy brook reflects the day,
But chok'd with sedges, works its weedy way.
Along thy glades, a solitary guest,
The hollow-sounding bittern guards its nest;
Amidst thy desert walks the lapwing flies,
And tires their echoes with unvaried cries.
Sunk are thy bowers in shapeless ruin all,
And the long grass o'ertops the mould'ring wall;
And trembling, shrinking from the spoiler's hand,
Far, far away, thy children leave the land.

Ill fares the land, to hast'ning ills a prey,
Where wealth accumulates, and men decay:
Princes and lords may flourish, or may fade;
A breath can make them, as a breath has made;
But a bold peasantry, their country's pride,
When once destroy'd, can never be supplied.

A time there was, ere England's griefs began,
When every rood of ground maintain'd its man;
For him light labour spread her wholesome store,
Just gave what life requir'd, but gave no more:
His best companions, innocence and health;
And his best riches, ignorance of wealth.

But times are alter'd; trade's unfeeling train
Usurp the land and dispossess the swain;
Along the lawn, where scatter'd hamlets rose,
Unwieldy wealth, and cumbrous pomp repose;
And every want to opulence allied,
And every pang that folly pays to pride.

'DEAR HARP OF MY COUNTRY'

Dear Harp of my Country! in darkness I found thee,
  The cold chain of silence had hung o'er thee long,
When proudly, my own Island Harp, I unbound thee,
  And gave all thy chords to light, freedom, and song!

The warm lay of love and the light note of gladness
  Have waken'd thy fondest, thy liveliest thrill;
But, so oft hast thou echo'd the deep sigh of sadness,
  That ev'n in thy mirth it will steal from thee still.

Dear Harp of my Country! farewell to thy numbers,
  This sweet wreath of song is the last we shall twine!
Go, sleep with the sunshine of Fame on thy slumbers,
  Till touch'd by some hand less unworthy than mine;

If the pulse of the patriot, soldier, or lover,
  Have throbb'd at our lay, 'tis thy glory alone;
I was *but* as the wind, passing heedlessly over,
  And all the wild sweetness I wak'd was thy own.

THOMAS MOORE (1779–1852)   119

THE LAKE ISLE OF INNISFREE

I will arise and go now, and go to Innisfree,
And a small cabin build there, of clay and wattles made:
Nine bean-rows will I have there, a hive for the
    honey-bee,
And live alone in the bee-loud glade.

And I shall have some peace there, for peace comes
    dropping slow,
Dropping from the veils of the morning to where the
    cricket sings;
There midnight's all a glimmer, and noon a purple
    glow,
And evening full of the linnet's wings.

I will arise and go now, for always night and day
I hear lake water lapping with low sounds by the shore;
While I stand on the roadway, or on the pavements
    grey,
I hear it in the deep heart's core.

EPIC

I have lived in important places, times
When great events were decided, who owned
That half a rood of rock, a no-man's land
Surrounded by our pitchfork-armed claims.
I heard the Duffys shouting 'Damn your soul'
And old McCabe stripped to the waist, seen
Step the plot defying blue cast-steel –
'Here is the march along these iron stones'.
That was the year of the Munich bother. Which
Was more important? I inclined
To lose my faith in Ballyrush and Gortin
Till Homer's ghost came whispering to my mind
He said: I made the Iliad from such
A local row. Gods make their own importance.

BELFAST

The hard cold fire of the northerner
Frozen into his blood from the fire in his basalt
Glares from behind the mica of his eyes
And the salt carrion water brings him wealth.

Down there at the end of the melancholy lough
Against the lurid sky over the stained water
Where hammers clang murderously on the girders
Like crucifixes the gantries stand.

And in the marble stores rubber gloves like polyps
Cluster; celluloid, painted ware, glaring
Metal patents, parchment lampshades, harsh
Attempts at buyable beauty.

In the porch of the chapel before the garish Virgin
A shawled factory-woman as if shipwrecked there
Lies a bunch of limbs glimpsed in the cave of gloom
By us who walk in the street so buoyantly and glib.

Over which country of cowled and haunted faces
The sun goes down with a banging of Orange drums
While the male kind murders each its woman
To whose prayer for oblivion answers no Madonna.

DUBLIN

Grey brick upon brick,
Declamatory bronze
On sombre pedestals –
O'Connell, Grattan, Moore –
And the brewery tugs and the swans
On the balustraded stream
And the bare bones of a fanlight
Over a hungry door
And the air soft on the cheek
And porter running from the taps
With a head of yellow cream
And Nelson on his pillar
Watching his world collapse.

This never was my town,
I was not born or bred
Nor schooled here and she will not
Have me alive or dead
But yet she holds my mind
With her seedy elegance,
With her gentle veils of rain
And all her ghosts that walk
And all that hide behind
Her Georgian facades –
The catcalls and the pain,

The glamour of her squalor,
The bravado of her talk.

The lights jig in the river
With a concertina movement
And the sun comes up in the morning
Like barley-sugar on the water
And the mist on the Wicklow hills
Is close, as close
As the peasantry were to the landlord,
As the Irish to the Anglo-Irish,
As the killer is close one moment
To the man he kills,
Or as the moment itself
Is close to the next moment.

She is not an Irish town
And she is not English,
Historic with guns and vermin
And the cold renown
Of a fragment of Church latin,
Of an oratorical phrase.
But oh the days are soft,
Soft enough to forget
The lesson better learnt,
The bullet on the wet
Streets, the crooked deal,

The steel behind the laugh,
The Four Courts burnt.

Fort of the Dane,
Garrison of the Saxon,
Augustan capital
Of a Gaelic nation,
Appropriating all
The alien brought,
You give me time for thought
And by a juggler's trick
You poise the toppling hour –
O greyness run to flower,
Grey stone, grey water,
And brick upon grey brick.

THE FIELDS OF ATHENRY

By a lonely prison wall
I heard a young girl calling
Micheal they are taking you away
For you stole Trevelyn's corn
So the young might see the morn.
Now a prison ship lies waiting in the bay.

Low lie the Fields of Athenry
Where once we watched the small free birds fly.
Our love was on the wing
we had dreams and songs to sing
It's so lonely 'round the Fields of Athenry.

By a lonely prison wall
I heard a young man calling
Nothing matters Mary when you're free,
Against the Famine and the Crown
I rebelled they ran me down
Now you must raise our child with dignity.

Low lie the Fields of Athenry
Where once we watched the small free birds fly.
Our love was on the wing
we had dreams and songs to sing
It's so lonely, 'round the Fields of Athenry.

126

By a lonely harbour wall
She watched the last star falling
As that prison ship sailed out against the sky
Sure she'll wait and hope and pray
For her love in Botany Bay
It's so lonely 'round the Fields of Athenry.

Low lie the Fields of Athenry
Where once we watched the small free birds fly.
Our love was on the wing
we had dreams and songs to sing
It's so lonely 'round the Fields of Athenry.

ANAHORISH

My 'place of clear water',
the first hill in the world
where springs washed into
the shiny grass

and darkened cobbles
in the bed of the lane.
Anahorish, soft gradient
of consonant, vowel-meadow,

after-image of lamps
swung through the yards
on winter evenings.
With pails and barrows

those mound-dwellers
go waist-deep in mist
to break the light ice
at wells and dunghills.

THE LINEN INDUSTRY

Pulling up flax after the blue flowers have fallen
And laying our handfuls in the peaty water
To rot those grasses to the bone, or building stooks
That recall the skirts of an invisible dancer,

We become a part of the linen industry
And follow its processes to the grubby town
Where fields are compacted into window-boxes
And there is little room among the big machines.

But even in our attic under the skylight
We make love on a bleach green, the whole meadow
Draped with material turning white in the sun
As though snow reluctant to melt were our attire.

What's passion but a battering of stubborn stalks,
Then a gentle combing out of fibres like hair
And a weaving of these into christening robes,
Into garments for a marriage or funeral?

Since it's like a bereavement once the labour's done
To find ourselves last workers in a dying trade,
Let flax be our matchmaker, our undertaker,
The provider of sheets for whatever the bed –

And be shy of your breasts in the presence of death,
Say that you look more beautiful in linen
Wearing white petticoats, the bow on your bodice
A butterfly attending the embroidered flowers.

GLENGORMLEY

'Wonders are many and none is more wonderful
          than man'
Who has tamed the terrier, trimmed the hedge
And grasped the principle of the watering-can.
Clothes-pegs litter the window ledge
And the long ships lie in clover. Washing lines
Shake out white linen over the chalk thanes.

Now we are safe from monsters, and the giants
Who tore up sods twelve miles by six
And hurled them out to sea to become islands
Can worry us no more. The sticks
And stones that once broke bones will not now harm
A generation of such sense and charm.

Only words hurt us now. No saint or hero,
Landing at night from the conspiring seas,
Brings dangerous tokens to the new era –
Their sad names linger in the histories.
The unreconciled, in their metaphysical pain,
Dangle from lamp-posts in the dawn rain;

And much dies with them. I should rather praise
A worldly time under this worldly sky –
The terrier-taming, garden-watering days
Those heroes pictured as they struggled through
The quick noose of their finite being. By
Necessity, if not choice, I live here too.

DEREK MAHON (1941–)   131

THE STANDING TRAINS

. . . and I thought how wonderful to miss
one's connections;
soon I shall miss them
all the time
LOUIS MACNEICE: *The Strings are False*

From the windows of a standing train
you can judge the artwork of our poor Republic.
The prominent ruins that make Limerick Junction
seem like Dresden in 1945
and the beaten-up coaches at Mallow Station,
the rusted side-tracks at Charleville,
have taken years of independent thought.
It takes decades to destroy a system
of stations. On the other hand, a few
well-placed hand-signals can destroy a whole
mode of life, a network of happiness.
This is our own Republic! O Memory,
O Patria, the shame of silenced junctions.
Time knew we'd rip the rails apart, we'd sell
emigrant tickets even while stripping
the ticket-office bare. The standing trains
of the future were backed against a wall.

Two hens peck seed from the bright platform,
hens roost in the signal-box.
Bilingual signs that caused a debate in the Senate
have been unbolted and used as gates:
it's late summer now in this dead station.
When I was twelve they unbolted the rails.
Now there's only the ghost of my father,
standing by the parcel-shed with his ghostly
suitcase. When he sees me walking towards him
he becomes upset. *Don't stop here!* he cries.
Keep going, keep going! This place is dead.

BELFAST CONFETTI

Suddenly as the riot squad moved in, it was raining
    exclamation marks,
Nuts, bolts, nails, car-keys. A fount of broken type.
    And the explosion
Itself – an asterisk on the map. This hyphenated line,
    a burst of rapid fire...
I was trying to complete a sentence in my head, but it
    kept stuttering,
All the alleyways and side-streets blocked with stops
    and colons.

I know this labyrinth so well – Balaclava, Raglan,
    Inkerman, Odessa Street –
Why can't I escape? Every move is punctuated.
    Crimea Street. Dead end again.
A Saracen, Kremlin-2 mesh. Makrolon face-shields.
    Walkie-talkies. What is
My name? Where am I coming from? Where am I
    going? A fusillade of question-marks.

EXPERIENCE
MATTERS

TO A HEDGEHOG

Thou grimmest far o grusome tykes
Grubbin thy food by thorny dykes
Gude faith, thou disna want for pikes
    Baith sharp an rauckle;[1]
Thou looks (Lord save's) arrayed in spikes,
    A creepin heckle.

Sure Nick begat thee, at the first,
On some auld whin or thorn accurst;
An some horn-fingered harpie nurst
    The ugly urchin;
Then Belzie, laughin like to burst,
    First caad thee hurchin.[2]

Fowk tell how thou, sae far frae daft,
Whan wind-faan fruit be scattered saft,
Will row thysel wi cunning craft
    An bear awa
Upon thy back, what fares thee aft,
    A day or twa.

But whether this account be true
Is mair than I will here avow;
If that thou stribs the outler cow,
    As some assert,
A pretty milkmaid, I allow,
    Forsooth thou art.

1 *rauckle*: strong   2 *hurchin*: hedgehog

Now creep awa the way ye came,
And tend your squeakin pups at hame;
Gin Colly should oerhear the same,
    It might be fatal,
For you, wi aa the pikes ye claim,
    Wi him to battle.

From THE IRISH COTTIER'S DEATH
AND BURIAL

> *'Nurs'd in the peasant's lowly shed,*
> *To hardy independence bravely bred;*
> *By early poverty to hardship steel'd,*
> *And train'd to arms in stern misfortune's field.'*
>
> ROBERT BURNS

Erin! my country! Preciously adorn'd
　　With every beauty, and with every worth,
Thy grievances through time shall not be scorn'd,
　　For powerful friends to plead thy cause step forth:
　　But more unblest, oppression, want and dearth,
Did during life, distressingly attend
　　The poor neglected native of thy North,
Whose fall I sing. He found no powerful friend,
'Til Death was sent by Heaven to bid his soul ascend.

The blameless Cottier, wha his youth had pass'd,
　　In temperance, an' felt few pains when auld,
The prey o' pleurisy, lies low at last,
　　And aft his thoughts are by delirium thrall'd:
　　Yet while he raves, he prays in words weel wal'd,
An' mutters through his sleep o' truth and right;
　　An' after pondering deep, the weans are tald
The readiest way he thinks they justly might
Support themselves thro' life, when he shall sink
　　　　in night.

Wi' patient watchfu'ness, lasses and lads,
    Carefu' an kin', surround his clean caff bed,
Ane to his lips the coolin' cordial ha'ds,
    An' ane behin' supports his achin' head;
    Some bin' the arm that lately has been bled,
An' some burn bricks his feet mair warm to make;
    If e'er he doze, how noiselessly they tread!
An' stap the lights to mak the bield be black,
An' aft beside lea, an' aft slip saftly back.

''TIS THE LAST ROSE OF SUMMER'

'Tis the last rose of summer
   Left blooming alone;
All her lovely companions
   Are faded and gone;
No flower of her kindred,
   No rose-bud is nigh,
To reflect back her blushes,
   Or give sigh for sigh.

I'll not leave thee, thou lone one!
   To pine on the stem;
Since the lovely are sleeping,
   Go, sleep thou with them.
Thus kindly I scatter
   Thy leaves o'er the bed,
Where thy mates of the garden
   Lie scentless and dead.

So soon may *I* follow,
   When friendships decay,
And from Love's shining circle
   The gems drop away.
When true hearts lie wither'd,
   And fond ones are flown,
Oh! who would inhabit
   This bleak world alone?

THOMAS MOORE (1779–1852)   141

DARK ROSALEEN

O my Dark Rosaleen,
   Do not sigh, do not weep!
The priests are on the ocean green,
   They march along the Deep.
There's wine ... from the royal Pope
   Upon the ocean green;
And Spanish ale shall give you hope,
   My Dark Rosaleen!
   My own Rosaleen!
Shall glad your heart, shall give you hope,
Shall give you health, and help, and hope,
   My Dark Rosaleen.

Over hills and through dales,
   Have I roamed for your sake;
All yesterday I sailed with sails
   On river and on lake.
The Erne ... at its highest flood
   I dashed across unseen,
For there was lightning in my blood,
   My Dark Rosaleen!
   My own Rosaleen!
Oh! there was lightning in my blood,
Red lightning lightened through my blood,
   My Dark Rosaleen!

All day long in unrest
    To and fro do I move,
The very soul within my breast
    Is wasted for you, love!
The heart...in my bosom faints
    To think of you, my Queen,
My life of life, my saint of saints,
    My Dark Rosaleen!
    My own Rosaleen!
To hear your sweet and sad complaints,
My life, my love, my saint of saints,
    My Dark Rosaleen!

Woe and pain, pain and woe,
    Are my lot night and noon,
To see your bright face clouded so,
    Like to the mournful moon.
But yet...will I rear your throne
    Again in golden sheen;
'Tis you shall reign, shall reign alone,
    My Dark Rosaleen!
    My own Rosaleen!
'Tis you shall have the golden throne,
'Tis you shall reign, and reign alone,
    My Dark Rosaleen!

Over dews, over sands
   Will I fly for your weal;
Your holy delicate white hands
   Shall girdle me with steel.
At home...in your emerald bowers,
   From morning's dawn till e'en,
You'll pray for me, my flower of flowers,
   My Dark Rosaleen!
   My fond Rosaleen!
You'll think of me through daylight's hours,
My virgin flower, my flower of flowers,
   My Dark Rosaleen!

I could scale the blue air,
   I could plough the high hills,
Oh, I could kneel all night in prayer,
   To heal your many ills!
And one...beamy smile from you
   Would float like light between
My toils and me, my own, my true,
   My Dark Rosaleen!
   My fond Rosaleen!
Would give me life and soul anew,
A second life, a soul anew,
   My Dark Rosaleen!

O! the Erne shall run red
  With redundance of blood,
The earth shall rock beneath our tread,
  And flames wrap hill and wood,
And gun-peal, and slogan cry,
  Wake many a glen serene,
Ere you shall fade, ere you shall die,
  My Dark Rosaleen!
  My own Rosaleen!
The Judgment Hour must first be nigh,
Ere you can fade, ere you can die,
  My Dark Rosaleen!

JAMES CLARENCE MANGAN (1803–49)

FROM THE IRISH OF COSTELLO

THE NAMELESS ONE

Roll forth, my song, like the rushing river
   That sweeps along to the mighty sea;
God will inspire me while I deliver
          My soul of thee!

Tell thou the world, when my bones lie whitening
   Amid the lost homes of youth and eld,
That there was once one whose veins ran lightning
          No eye beheld.

Tell how his boyhood was one drear night-hour,
   How shone for him, through his griefs and gloom,
No star of all Heaven sends to light our
          Path to the tomb.

Roll on, my song, and to after ages
   Tell how, disdaining all earth can give,
He would have taught men, from Wisdom's pages,
          The way to live.

And tell how trampled, derided, hated,
   And worn by weakness, disease, and wrong,
He fled for shelter to God, who mated
          His soul with song –

With song which always, sublime or vapid,
    Flowed like a rill in the morning-beam,
Perchance not deep, but intense and rapid –
        A mountain stream.

Tell how this Nameless, condemned for years long
    To herd with demons from Hell beneath,
Saw things that made him, with groans and tears, long
        For even death.

Go on to tell how, with genius wasted,
    Betrayed in friendship, befooled in love,
With spirit shipwrecked, and young hopes blasted,
        He still, still strove.

Till, spent with toil, dreeing death for others,
    And some whose hands should have wrought
      for him;
(If children live not for sires and mothers),
        His mind grew dim.

And he fell far through that pit abysmal,
    The gulf and grave of Maginn and Burns,
And pawned his soul for the devil's dismal
        Stock of returns.

But yet redeemed it in days of darkness,
  And shapes and signs of the final wrath,
When death, in hideous and ghastly starkness,
        Stood on his path.

And tell how now, amid wreck and sorrow,
  And want, and sickness, and houseless nights,
He bides in calmness the silent morrow,
        That no ray lights.

And lives he still, then? Yes! Old and hoary
  At thirty-nine, from despair and woe,
He lives, enduring what future story
        Will never know.

Him grant a grave to, ye pitying noble,
  Deep in your bosoms! There let him dwell!
He, too, had tears for all souls in trouble,
        Here and in Hell.

GOOD COUNSEL
(*from the Ottoman*)

Tutor not thyself in science: go to masters for perfection;
     Also speak thy thoughts aloud:
Whoso in the glass beholdeth nought besides his own
    reflection
     Bides both ignorant and proud.

Study not in one book only: bee-like, rather, at a hundred
     Sources gather honeyed lore:
Thou art else that helpless bird which, when her nest
    has once been plundered,
     Ne'er can build another more.

From THE BALLAD OF
READING GAOL

He did not wear his scarlet coat,
    For blood and wine are red,
And blood and wine were on his hands
    When they found him with the dead,
The poor dead woman whom he loved,
    And murdered in her bed.

He walked amongst the Trial Men
    In a suit of shabby gray;
A cricket cap was on his head,
    And his step seemed light and gay;
But I never saw a man who looked
    So wistfully at the day.

I never saw a man who looked
    With such a wistful eye
Upon that little tent of blue
    Which prisoners call the sky,
And at every drifting cloud that went
    With sails of silver by.

I walked with other souls in pain,
    Within another ring,
And was wondering if the man had done

A great or little thing,
When a voice behind me whispered low,
 'That fellow's got to swing.'

Dear Christ! the very prison walls
  Suddenly seemed to reel,
And the sky above my head became
  Like a casque of scorching steel;
And, though I was a soul in pain,
  My pain I could not feel.

I only knew what hunted thought
  Quickened his step, and why
He looked upon the garish day
  With such a wistful eye;
The man had killed the thing he loved,
  And so he had to die.

*   *   *

Yet each man kills the thing he loves,
  By each let this be heard,
Some do it with a bitter look,
  Some with a flattering word,
The coward does it with a kiss,
  The brave man with a sword!

Some kill their love when they are young,
    And some when they are old;
Some strangle with the hands of Lust,
    Some with the hands of Gold:
The kindest use a knife, because
    The dead so soon grow cold.

Some love too little, some too long,
    Some sell, and others buy;
Some do the deed with many tears,
    And some without a sigh:
For each man kills the thing he loves,
    Yet each man does not die.

He does not die a death of shame
    On a day of dark disgrace,
Nor have a noose about his neck,
    Nor a cloth upon his face,
Nor drop feet foremost through the floor
    Into an empty space.

JUNE

Broom out the floor now, lay the fender by,
And plant this bee-sucked bough of woodbine there,
And let the window down. The butterfly
Floats in upon the sunbeam, and the fair
Tanned face of June, the nomad gipsy, laughs
Above her widespread wares, the while she tells
The farmers' fortunes in the fields, and quaffs
The water from the spider-peopled wells.

The hedges are all drowned in green grass seas,
And bobbing poppies flare like Elmo's light,
While siren-like the pollen-stained bees
Drone in the clover depths. And up the height
The cuckoo's voice is hoarse and broke with joy.
And on the lowland crops the crows make raid,
Nor fear the clappers of the farmer's boy,
Who sleeps, like drunken Noah, in the shade.

And loop this red rose in that hazel ring
That snares your little ear, for June is short
And we must joy in it and dance and sing.
And from her bounty draw her rosy worth.
Ay! soon the swallows will be flying south,
The wind wheel north to gather in the snow,
Even the roses split on youth's red mouth
Will soon blow down the road all roses go.

FRANCIS LEDWIDGE (1891–1917)   153

THE STOLEN CHILD

Where dips the rocky highland
Of Sleuth Wood in the lake,
There lies a leafy island
Where flapping herons wake
The drowsy water-rats;
There we've hid our faery vats,
Full of berries
And of reddest stolen cherries.
Come away, O human child!
To the waters and the wild
With a faery, hand in hand,
For the world's more full of weeping than you can
understand.

Where the wave of moonlight glosses
The dim grey sands with light,
Far off by furthest Rosses
We foot it all the night,
Weaving olden dances,
Mingling hands and mingling glances
Till the moon has taken flight;
To and fro we leap
And chase the frothy bubbles,
While the world is full of troubles
And is anxious in its sleep.

Come away, O human child!
To the waters and the wild
With a faery, hand in hand,
For the world's more full of weeping than you can
        understand.

Where the wandering water gushes
From the hills above Glen-Car,
In pools among the rushes
That scarce could bathe a star,
We seek for slumbering trout
And whispering in their ears
Give them unquiet dreams;
Leaning softly out
From ferns that drop their tears
Over the young streams.
Come away, O human child!
To the waters and the wild
With a faery, hand in hand,
For the world's more full of weeping than you can
        understand.

Away with us he's going,
The solemn-eyed:
He'll hear no more the lowing

Of the calves on the warm hillside
Or the kettle on the hob
Sing peace into his breast,
Or see the brown mice bob
Round and round the oatmeal-chest.
For he comes, the human child,
To the waters and the wild
With a faery, hand in hand,
From a world more full of weeping than he can
understand.

DOWN BY THE SALLEY GARDENS

Down by the salley gardens my love and I did meet;
She passed the salley gardens with little
    snow-white feet.
She bid me take love easy, as the leaves grow
    on the tree;
But I, being young and foolish, with her would
    not agree.

In a field by the river my love and I did stand,
And on my leaning shoulder she laid her
    snow-white hand.
She bid me take life easy, as the grass grows
    on the weirs;
But I was young and foolish, and now am full of tears.

W. B. YEATS (1865–1939)

TO A WEALTHY MAN WHO PROMISED
A SECOND SUBSCRIPTION TO THE
DUBLIN MUNICIPAL GALLERY
IF IT WERE PROVED THE PEOPLE
WANTED PICTURES

You gave, but will not give again
Until enough of Paudeen's pence
By Biddy's halfpennies have lain
To be 'some sort of evidence',
Before you'll put your guineas down,
That things it were a pride to give
Are what the blind and ignorant town
Imagines best to make it thrive.
What cared Duke Ercole, that bid
His mummers to the market-place,
What th' onion-sellers thought or did
So that his Plautus set the pace
For the Italian comedies?
And Guidobaldo, when he made
That grammar school of courtesies
Where wit and beauty learned their trade
Upon Urbino's windy hill,
Had sent no runners to and fro
That he might learn the shepherds' will.
And when they drove out Cosimo,
Indifferent how the rancour ran,

He gave the hours they had set free
To Michelozzo's latest plan
For the San Marco Library,
Whence turbulent Italy should draw
Delight in Art whose end is peace,
In logic and in natural law
By sucking at the dugs of Greece.

Your open hand but shows our loss,
For he knew better how to live.
Let Paudeens play at pitch and toss,
Look up in the sun's eye and give
What the exultant heart calls good
That some new day may breed the best
Because you gave, not what they would,
But the right twigs for an eagle's nest!

December 1912

W. B. YEATS (1865–1939)   159

AN IRISH AIRMAN FORESEES
HIS DEATH

I know that I shall meet my fate
Somewhere among the clouds above;
Those that I fight I do not hate,
Those that I guard I do not love;
My country is Kiltartan Cross,
My countrymen Kiltartan's poor,
No likely end could bring them loss
Or leave them happier than before.
Nor law, nor duty bade me fight,
Nor public men, nor cheering crowds,
A lonely impulse of delight
Drove to this tumult in the clouds;
I balanced all, brought all to mind,
The years to come seemed waste of breath,
A waste of breath the years behind
In balance with this life, this death.

THE SECOND COMING

Turning and turning in the widening gyre
The falcon cannot hear the falconer;
Things fall apart; the centre cannot hold;
Mere anarchy is loosed upon the world,
The blood-dimmed tide is loosed, and everywhere
The ceremony of innocence is drowned;
The best lack all conviction, while the worst
Are full of passionate intensity.
Surely some revelation is at hand;
Surely the Second Coming is at hand.
The Second Coming! Hardly are those words out
When a vast image out of *Spiritus Mundi*
Troubles my sight: somewhere in sands of the desert
A shape with lion body and the head of a man,
A gaze blank and pitiless as the sun,
Is moving its slow thighs, while all about it
Reel shadows of the indignant desert birds.
The darkness drops again; but now I know
That twenty centuries of stony sleep
Were vexed to nightmare by a rocking cradle,
And what rough beast, its hour come round at last,
Slouches towards Bethlehem to be born?

w. b. yeats (1865–1939)   161

SAILING TO BYZANTIUM

I

That is no country for old men. The young
In one another's arms, birds in the trees,
– Those dying generations – at their song,
The salmon-falls, the mackerel-crowded seas,
Fish, flesh, or fowl, commend all summer long
Whatever is begotten, born, and dies.
Caught in that sensual music all neglect
Monuments of unageing intellect.

II

An aged man is but a paltry thing,
A tattered coat upon a stick, unless
Soul clap its hands and sing, and louder sing
For every tatter in its mortal dress,
Nor is there singing school but studying
Monuments of its own magnificence;
And therefore I have sailed the seas and come
To the holy city of Byzantium.

III

O sages standing in God's holy fire
As in the gold mosaic of a wall,
Come from the holy fire, perne in a gyre,
And be the singing-masters of my soul.

Consume my heart away; sick with desire
And fastened to a dying animal
It knows not what it is; and gather me
Into the artifice of eternity.

IV

Once out of nature I shall never take
My bodily form from any natural thing,
But such a form as Grecian goldsmiths make
Of hammered gold and gold enamelling
To keep a drowsy Emperor awake;
Or set upon a golden bough to sing
To lords and ladies of Byzantium
Of what is past, or passing, or to come.

W. B. YEATS (1865–1939)

ECCE PUER

Of the dark past
A child is born
With joy and grief
My heart is torn.

Calm in his cradle
The living lies.
May love and mercy
Unclose his eyes!

Young life is breathed
On the glass;
The world that was not
Comes to pass.

A child is sleeping:
An old man gone.
O, father forsaken,
Forgive your son!

MEMORY OF MY FATHER

Every old man I see
Reminds me of my father
When he had fallen in love with death
One time when sheaves were gathered.

That man I saw in Gardner Street
Stumble on the kerb was one,
He stared at me half-eyed,
I might have been his son.

And I remember the musician
Faltering over his fiddle
In Bayswater, London,
He too set me the riddle.

Every old man I see
In October-coloured weather
Seems to say to me:
'I was once your father.'

PATRICK KAVANAGH (1904–67)

PRELUDE

Give us another poem, he said
Or they will think your muse is dead;
Another middle-age departure
Of Apollo from the trade of archer.
Bring out a book as soon as you can
To let them see you're a living man,
Whose comic spirit is untamed
Though sadness for a little claimed
The precedence; and tentative
You pulled your punch and wondered if
Old Cunning Silence might not be
A better bet than poetry.

You have not got the countenance
To hold the angle of pretence,
That angry bitter look for one
Who knows that art's a kind of fun;
That all true poems laugh inwardly
Out of grief-born intensity.
Dullness alone can get you beat
And so can humour's counterfeit.
You have not got a chance with fraud
And might as well be true to God.

Then link your laughter out of doors
In sunlight past the sick-faced whores
Who chant the praise of love that isn't
And bring their bastards to be Christened
At phoney founts by bogus priests
With rites mugged up by journalists
Walk past professors looking serious
Fondling an unpublished thesis –
'A child! my child! my darling son'
Some Poets of Nineteen Hundred and One.

Note well the face profoundly grave,
An empty mind can house a knave.
Be careful to show no defiance,
They've made pretence into a science;
Card-sharpers of the art committee
Working all the provincial cities,
They cry 'Eccentric' if they hear
A voice that seems at all sincere.
Fold up their table and their gear
And with the money disappear.

But satire is unfruitful prayer,
Only wild shoots of pity there,
And you must go inland and be
Lost in compassion's ecstasy,

Where suffering soars in summer air –
The millstone has become a star.

Count then your blessings, hold in mind
All that has loved you or been kind:
Those women on their mercy missions,
Rescue work with kiss or kitchens,
Perceiving through the comic veil
The poet's spirit in travail.
Gather the bits of road that were
Not gravel to the traveller
But eternal lanes of joy
On which no man who walks can die.
Bring in the particular trees
That caught you in their mysteries,
And love again the weeds that grew
Somewhere specially for you.
Collect the river and the stream
That flashed upon a pensive theme,
And a positive world make,
A world man's world cannot shake.
And do not lose love's resolution
Though face to face with destitution.
If Platitude should claim a place
Do not denounce his humble face;
His sentiments are well intentioned
He has a part in the larger legend.

So now my gentle tiger burning
In the forest of no-yearning
Walk on serenely, do not mind
That Promised Land you thought to find,
Where the worldly-wise and rich take over
The mundane problems of the lower,
Ignore Power's schismatic sect,
Lovers alone lovers protect.

GNOME

Spend the years of learning squandering
Courage for the years of wandering
Through the world politely turning
From the loutishness of learning

CHRYSALIDES

Our last free summer we mooned about at odd hours
Pedalling slowly through country towns, stopping
    to eat
Chocolate and fruit, tracing our vagaries on the map.

At night we watched in the barn, to the lurch of
    melodeon music,
The crunching boots of countrymen – huge and
    weightless
As their shadows – twirling and leaping over the
    yellow concrete.

Sleeping too little or too much, we awoke at noon
And were received with womanly mockery into the
    kitchen,
Like calves poking our faces in with enormous hunger.

Daily we strapped our saddlebags and went to
    experience
A tolerance we shall never know again, confusing
For the last time, for example, the licit and the familiar.

Our instincts blurred with change; a strange
    wakefulness
Sapped our energies and dulled our slow-beating hearts
To the extremes of feeling – insensitive alike

To the unique succession of our youthful midnights,
When by a window ablaze softly with the virgin moon
Dry scones and jugs of milk awaited us in the dark,

Or to lasting horror: a wedding flight of ants
Spawning to its death, a mute perspiration
Glistening like drops of copper in our path.

'LIKE DOLMENS ROUND MY CHILDHOOD, THE OLD PEOPLE'

Like dolmens round my childhood, the old people.

Jamie MacCrystal sang to himself,
A broken song without tune, without words;
He tipped me a penny every pension day,
Fed kindly crusts to winter birds.
When he died, his cottage was robbed,
Mattress and money box torn and searched.
Only the corpse they didn't disturb.

Maggie Owens was surrounded by animals,
A mongrel bitch and shivering pups,
Even in her bedroom a she-goat cried.
She was a well of gossip defiled,
Fanged chronicler of a whole countryside:
Reputed a witch, all I could find
Was her lonely need to deride.

The Nialls lived along a mountain lane
Where heather bells bloomed, clumps of foxglove.
All were blind, with Blind Pension and Wireless,
Dead eyes serpent-flicked as one entered
To shelter from a downpour of mountain rain.
Crickets chirped under the rocking hearthstone
Until the muddy sun shone out again.

Mary Moore lived in a crumbling gatehouse,
Famous as Pisa for its leaning gable.
Bag-apron and boots, she tramped the fields
Driving lean cattle from a miry stable.
A by-word for fierceness, she fell asleep
Over love stories, Red Star and Red Circle,
Dreamed of gypsy love rites, by firelight sealed.

Wild Billy Eagleson married a Catholic servant girl
When all his Loyal family passed on:
We danced round him shouting 'To Hell with King
     Billy',
And dodged from the arc of his flailing blackthorn.
Forsaken by both creeds, he showed little concern
Until the Orange drums banged past in the summer
And bowler and sash aggressively shone.

Curate and doctor trudged to attend them,
Through knee-deep snow, through summer heat,
From main road to lane to broken path,
Gulping the mountain air with painful breath.
Sometimes they were found by neighbours,
Silent keepers of a smokeless hearth,
Suddenly cast in the mould of death.

Ancient Ireland, indeed! I was reared by her bedside,
The rune and the chant, evil eye and averted head,
Fomorian fierceness of family and local feud.
Gaunt figures of fear and of friendliness,
For years they trespassed on my dreams,
Until once, in a standing circle of stones,
I felt their shadows pass

Into that dark permanence of ancient forms.

11 RUE DAGUERRE

At night, sometimes, when I cannot sleep
I go to the *atelier* door
And smell the earth of the garden.

It exhales softly,
Especially now, approaching springtime,
When tendrils of green are plaited

Across the humus, desperately frail
In their passage against
The dark, unredeemed parcels of earth.

There is white light on the cobblestones
And in the apartment house opposite –
All four floors – silence.

In that stillness – soft but luminously exact,
A chosen light – I notice that
The tips of the lately grafted cherry-tree

Are a firm and lacquered black.

THERE WILL BE A TALKING

There will be a talking of lovely things
there will be cognizance of the seasons,
there will be men who know the flights of birds,
in new days there will be love for women:
we will walk the balance of artistry.
And things will have a middle and an end,
and be loved because being beautiful.
Who in a walk will find a lasting vase
depicting dance and hold it in his hands
and sell it then? No man on the new earth
will barter with malice nor make of stone
a hollowed riddle: for art will be art,
the freak, the rare no longer commonplace:
there will be a going back to the laws.

MICHAEL HARTNETT (1941–)   177

SEALS AT HIGH ISLAND

The calamity of seals begins with jaws.
Born in caverns that reverberate
With endless malice of the sea's tongue
Clacking on shingle, they learn to bark back
In fear and sadness and celebration.
The ocean's mouth opens forty feet wide
And closes on a morsel of their rock.

Swayed by the thrust and backfall of the tide,
A dappled grey bull and a brindled cow
Copulate in the green water of a cove.
I watch from a cliff-top, trying not to move.
Sometimes they sink and merge into black shoals;
Then rise for air, his muzzle on her neck,
Their winged feet intertwined as a fishtail.

She opens her fierce mouth like a scarlet flower
Full of white seeds; she holds it open long
At the sunburst in the music of their loving;
And cries a little. But I must remember
How far their feelings are from mine marooned.
If there are tears at this holy ceremony
Theirs are caused by brine and mine by breeze.

When the great bull withdraws his rod, it glows
Like a carnelian candle set in jade.
The cow ripples ashore to feed her calf;
While an old rival, eyeing the deed with hate,
Swims to attack the tired triumphant god.
They rear their heads above the boiling surf,
Their terrible jaws open, jetting blood.

At nightfall they haul out, and mourn the drowned,
Playing to the sea sadly their last quartet,
An improvised requiem that ravishes
Reason, while ripping scale up like a net:
Brings pity trembling down the rocky spine
Of headlands, till the bitter ocean's tongue
Swells in their cove, and smothers their sweet song.

SNOW

The room was suddenly rich and the great
    bay-window was
Spawning snow and pink roses against it
Soundlessly collateral and incompatible:
World is suddener than we fancy it.

World is crazier and more of it than we think,
Incorrigibly plural. I peel and portion
A tangerine and spit the pips and feel
The drunkenness of things being various.

And the fire flames with a bubbling sound for world
Is more spiteful and gay than one supposes –
On the tongue on the eyes on the ears in the palms
    of one's hands –
There is more than glass between the snow and the
    huge roses.

WOLVES

I do not want to be reflective any more
Envying and despising unreflective things
Finding pathos in dogs and undeveloped handwriting
And young girls doing their hair and all the castles
    of sand
Flushed by the children's bedtime, level with the shore.

The tide comes in and goes out again, I do not want
To be always stressing either its flux or its permanence,
I do not want to be a tragic or philosophic chorus
But to keep my eye only on the nearer future
And after that let the sea flow over us.

Come then all of you, come closer, form a circle,
Join hands and make believe that joined
Hands will keep away the wolves of water
Who howl along our coast. And be it assumed
That no one hears them among the talk and laughter.

LOUIS MacNEICE (1907–63)   181

IN MEMORIAM

My father, let no similes eclipse
Where crosses like some forest simplified
Sink roots into my mind; the slow sands
Of your history delay till through your eyes
I read you like a book. Before you died,
Re-enlisting with all the broken soldiers
You bent beneath your rucksack, near collapse,
In anecdote rehearsed and summarized
These words I write in memory. Let yours
And other heartbreaks play into my hands.

Now I see in close-up, in my mind's eye,
The cracked and splintered dead for pity's sake
Each dismal evening predecease the sun,
You, looking death and nightmare in the face
With your kilt, harmonica and gun,
Grow older in a flash, but none the wiser
(Who, following the wrong queue at The Palace,
Have joined the London Scottish by mistake),
Your nineteen years uncertain if and why
Belgium put the kibosh on the Kaiser.

Between the corpses and the soup canteens
You swooned away, watching your future spill.
But, as it was, your proper funeral urn

Had mercifully smashed to smithereens,
To shrapnel shards that sliced your testicle.
That instant I, your most unlikely son,
In No Man's Land was surely left for dead,
Blotted out from your far horizon.
As your voice now is locked inside my head,
I yet was held secure, waiting my turn.

Finally, that lousy war was over.
Stranded in France and in need of proof
You hunted down experimental lovers,
Persuading chorus girls and countesses:
This, father, the last confidence you spoke.
In my twentieth year your old wounds woke
As cancer. Lodging under the same roof
Death was a visitor who hung about,
Strewing the house with pills and bandages,
Till he chose to put your spirit out.

Though they overslept the sequence of events
Which ended with the ambulance outside,
You lingering in the hall, your bowels on fire,
Tears in your eyes, and all your medals spent,
I summon girls who packed at last and went
Underground with you. Their souls again on hire,

Now those lost wives as recreated brides
Take shape before me, materialize.
On the verge of light and happy legend
They lift their skirts like blinds across your eyes.

MID-TERM BREAK

I sat all morning in the college sick bay
Counting bells knelling classes to a close.
At two o'clock our neighbours drove me home.

In the porch I met my father crying –
He had always taken funerals in his stride –
And Big Jim Evans saying it was a hard blow.

The baby cooed and laughed and rocked the pram
When I came in, and I was embarrassed
By old men standing up to shake my hand

And tell me they were 'sorry for my trouble'.
Whispers informed strangers I was the eldest,
Away at school, as my mother held my hand

In hers and coughed out angry tearless sighs.
At ten o'clock the ambulance arrived
With the corpse, stanched and bandaged by the nurses.

Next morning I went up into the room. Snowdrops
And candles soothed the bedside; I saw him
For the first time in six weeks. Paler now,

Wearing a poppy bruise on his left temple,
He lay in the four-foot box as in his cot.
No gaudy scars, the bumper knocked him clear.

A four-foot box, a foot for every year.

From CLEARANCES

When all the others were away at Mass
I was all hers as we peeled potatoes.
They broke the silence, let fall one by one
Like solder weeping off the soldering iron:
Cold comforts set between us, things to share
Gleaming in a bucket of clean water.
And again let fall. Little pleasant splashes
From each other's work would bring us to our senses.

So while the parish priest at her bedside
Went hammer and tongs at the prayers for the dying
And some were responding and some crying
I remembered her head bent towards my head,
Her breath in mine, our fluent dipping knives –
Never closer the whole rest of our lives.

THE UNDERGROUND
From STATION ISLAND

There we were in the vaulted tunnel running,
You in your going-away coat speeding ahead
And me, me then like a fleet god gaining
Upon you before you turned to a reed

Or some new white flower japped with crimson
As the coat flapped wild and button after button
Sprang off and fell in a trail
Between the Underground and the Albert Hall.

Honeymooning, mooning around, late for the Proms,
Our echoes die in that corridor and now
I come as Hansel came on the moonlit stones
Retracing the path back, lifting the buttons

To end up in a draughty lamplit station
After the trains have gone, the wet track
Bared and tensed as I am, all attention
For your step following and damned if I look back.

LONDON

At fifty, she misses the breast
That grew in her thirteenth year
And was removed last month. She misses
The small car she drove through the seaside town
And along cliffs for miles. In London
She will not take the tube, is afraid of taxis.

We choose a random bar. She sits by me,
Looking along the jacketed line of men's
Lunchtime backs, drinks her vermouth.
I see her eye slide to the left;
At the counter's end sits a high metal urn.

What are you staring at? That polished curve,
The glint wavering on steel, the features
Of our stranger neighbour distorted.
You can't see it from where you are.
When that streak of crooked light
Goes out, my life is over.

EILÉAN NÍ CHUILLEANÁIN (1942–)   189

SO SHE LOOKED, IN THAT COMPANY

Seeing her here
I know at once who she must be.
She does not move while
The pale figures out of the anthologies
In their coarse shirts are paraded
To tell their hesitant stories
Twisting the grammar of their exotic speech.

They line up as if
Back to the wall were the only possible stance.
Their throats are scarred and their voices
Birdlike.
     – Until the viewing is over,
The woman waits to be taken away,
Then they can be heard, heartily chatting
Among themselves, calling for big jugs of drink.

IN HER OWN IMAGE

It is her eyes:
the irises are gold
and round they go
like the ring on my wedding finger,
round and round

and I can't touch
their histories or tears.
To think they were once my satellites!
They shut me out now.
Such light years!

She is not myself
anymore, she is not
even in my sky
anymore and I
am not myself.

I will not disfigure
her pretty face.
Let her wear amethyst thumbprints,
a family heirloom,
a sort of burial necklace

and I know just the place:
Where the wall glooms,
where the lettuce seeds,
where the jasmine springs
no surprises

I will bed her.
She will bloom there,
second nature to me,
the one perfection
among compromises.

NIGHT FEED

This is dawn
Believe me
This is your season, little daughter.
The moment daisies open,
The hour mercurial rainwater
Makes a mirror for sparrows.
It's time we drowned our sorrows.

I tiptoe in.
I lift you up
Wriggling
In your rosy, zipped sleeper.
Yes, this is the hour
For the early bird and me
When finder is keeper.

I crook the bottle.
How you suckle!
This is the best I can be,
Housewife
To this nursery
Where you hold on,
Dear life.

A silt of milk.
The last suck
And now your eyes are open,
Birth-coloured and offended.
Earth wakes.
You go back to sleep.
The feed is ended.

Worms turn.
Stars go in.
Even the moon is losing face.
Poplars stilt for dawn
And we begin
The long fall from grace.
I tuck you in

NOCTURNE

After a friend has gone I like the feel of it:
The house at night. Everyone asleep.
The way it draws in like atmosphere or evening.

One-o-clock. A floral teapot and a raisin scone.
A tray waits to be taken down.
The landing light is off. The clock strikes. The cat

comes into his own, mysterious on the stairs,
a black ambivalence around the legs of button-back
chairs, an insinuation to be set beside

the red spoon and the salt-glazed cup,
the saucer with the thick spill of tea
which scalds off easily under the tap. Time

is a tick, a purr, a drop. The spider
on the dining room window has fallen asleep
among complexities as I will once

the doors are bolted and the keys tested
and the switch turned up of the kitchen light
which made outside in the back garden

an electric room – a domestication
of closed daisies, an architecture
instant and improbable.

EAVAN BOLAND (1944–)

TURN AGAIN

There is a map of the city which shows the bridge that
    was never built.
A map which shows the bridge that collapsed; the
    streets that never existed.
Ireland's Entry, Elbow Lane, Weigh-House Lane,
    Back Lane, Stone-Cutter's Entry –
Today's plan is already yesterday's – the streets that
    were there are gone.
And the shape of the jails cannot be shown for security
    reasons.

The linen backing is falling apart – the Falls Road
    hangs by a thread.
When someone asks me where I live, I remember
    where I used to live.
Someone asks me for directions, and I think again.
    I turn into
A side-street to try to throw off my shadow, and
    history is changed.

THE EXILES' CLUB

Every Thursday in the upstairs lounge of the
    Wollongong Bar, they make
Themselves at home with Red Heart Stout, Park
    Drive cigarettes and Dunville's whiskey,
A slightly-mouldy batch of soda farls. Eventually, they
    get down to business.
After years they have reconstructed the whole of the
    Falls Road, and now
Are working on the back streets: Lemon, Peel and
    Omar, Balaclava, Alma.

They just about keep up with the news of bombings
    and demolition, and are
Struggling with the finer details: the names and dates
    carved out
On the back bench of the Leavers' Class in Slate Street
    School; the Nemo Café menu;
The effects of the 1941 Blitz, the entire contents of
    Paddy Lavery's pawnshop.

CIARAN CARSON (1948–)   197

THE 'SINGER'

In the evenings I used to study
at my mother's old sewing-machine,
pressing my feet occasionally
up and down on the treadle
as though I were going somewhere
I had never been.

Every year at exams, the pressure mounted –
the summer light bent across my pages
like a squinting eye. The children's shouts
echoed the weather of the street,
a car was thunder,
the ticking of a clock was heavy rain . . .

In the dark I drew the curtains
on young couples stopping in the entry,
heading home. There were nights
I sent the disconnected wheel
spinning madly round and round
till the empty bobbin rattled in its case.

THE FLOWER MASTER

Like foxgloves in the school of the grass moon
we come to terms with shade, with the principle
of enfolding space. Our scissors in brocade,
we learn the coolness of straight edges, how
to stroke gently the necks of daffodils
and make them throw their heads back to the sun.

We slip the thready stems of violets, delay
the loveliness of the hibiscus dawn with quiet ovals,
spirals of feverfew like water splashing,
the papery legacies of bluebells. We do
sea-fans with sea-lavender, moon-arrangements
roughly for the festival of moon-viewing.

This black container calls for sloes, sweet
sultan, dainty nipplewort, in honour
of a special guest who, summoned to the
tea ceremony, must stoop to our low doorway,
our fontanelle, the trout's dimpled feet.

MEDBH McGUCKIAN (1950–)

THE SITTING

My half-sister comes to me to be painted:
She is posing furtively, like a letter being
Pushed under a door, making a tunnel with her
Hands over her dull-rose dress. Yet her coppery
Head is as bright as a net of lemons. I am
Painting it hair by hair as if she had not
Disowned it, or forsaken those unsparkling
Eyes as blue may be sifted from the surface
Of a cloud; and she questions my brisk
Brushwork, the note of positive red
In the kissed mouth I have given her,
As a woman's touch makes curtains blossom
Permanently in a house: she calls it
Wishfulness, the failure of the tampering rain
To go right into the mountain, she prefers
My sea-studies, and will not sit for me
Again, something half-opened, rarer
Than railroads, a soiled red-letter day.

QUOOF

How often have I carried our family word
for the hot water bottle
to a strange bed,
as my father would juggle a red-hot half-brick
in an old sock
to his childhood settle.
I have taken it into so many lovely heads
or laid it between us like a sword.

An hotel room in New York City
with a girl who spoke hardly any English,
my hand on her breast
like the smouldering one-off spoor of the yeti
or some other shy beast
that has yet to enter the language.

SYMPOSIUM

You can lead a horse to water but you can't make it hold
its nose to the grindstone and hunt with the hounds.
Every dog has a stitch in time. Two heads? You've
    been sold
one good turn. One good turn deserves a bird in
    the hand.

A bird in the hand is better than no bread.
To have your cake is to pay Paul.
Make hay while you can still hit the nail on the head.
For want of a nail the sky might fall.

People in glass houses can't see the wood
for the new broom. Rome wasn't built between
    two stools.
Empty vessels wait for no man.

A hair of the dog is a friend indeed.
There's no fool like the fool
who's shot his bolt. There's no smoke after the horse
    is gone.

THE FULL INDIAN ROPE TRICK

There was no secret
murmured down through a long line
of elect; no dark fakir, no flutter
of notes from a pipe,
no proof, no footage of it –
but I did it,

Guildhall Square, noon,
in front of everyone.
There were walls, bells, passers-by;
then a rope, thrown, caught by the sky
and me, young, up and away,
goodbye.

Goodbye, goodbye.
Thin air. First try.
A crowd hushed, squinting eyes
at a full sun. There
on the stones
the slack weight of a rope

coiled in a crate, a braid
eighteen summers long,
and me
I'm long gone,
my one-off trick
unique, unequalled since.

And what would I tell them
given the chance?
It was painful; it took years.
I'm my own witness,
guardian of the fact
that I'm still here.

THE ULSTER WAY

This is not about burns or hedges.
There will be no gorse. You will not
notice the ceaseless photosynthesis
or the dead tree's thousand fingers,
the trunk's inhumanity writhing with texture,
as you will not be passing into farmland.
Nor will you be set upon by cattle,

ingleberried, haunching and haunting
with their eyes, their shocking opals,
graving you, hoovering and scooping you,
full of a whatness that sieves you through
the abattoir hillscape, the runnel's slabber
through darkgrass, sweating for the night
that will purple to a love-bitten bruise.

All this is in your head. If you walk,
don't walk away, in silence, under the stars'
ice-fires of violence, to the water's darkened strand.
For this is not about horizons, or their curving
limitations. This is not about the rhythm
of a songline. There are other paths to follow.
Everything is about you. Now listen.

ALAN GILLIS (1973–)   205

POETRY

It's a bit like looking through the big window
on the top deck of the number 47.

I'm watching you, and her, and all of them,
but through my own reflection.

Or opening my eyes when everyone's praying.
The wave machine of my father's breathing,

my mother's limestone-fingered steeple,
my sister's tiny fidgets, and me, moon-eyed,
     unforgetting.

And then the oak doors flapping slowly open to
     let us out,
like some great injured bird trying to take flight.

LOVE MATTERS

'IS IT A MONTH'

Is it a month since I and you
In the starlight of Glen Dubh
Stretched beneath a hazel bough
Kissed from ear and throat to brow,
Since your fingers, neck, and chin
Made the bars that fenced me in,
Till Paradise seemed but a wreck
Near your bosom, brow, and neck
And stars grew wilder, growing wise,
In the splendour of your eyes!
Since the weasel wandered near
Whilst we kissed from ear to ear
And the wet and withered leaves
Blew about your cap and sleeves,
Till the moon sank tired through the ledge
Of the wet and windy hedge?
And we took the starry lane
Back to Dublin town again.

J. M. SYNGE (1871–1909)

HE WISHES FOR THE
CLOTHS OF HEAVEN

Had I the heavens' embroidered cloths,
Enwrought with golden and silverlight,
The blue and the dim and the dark cloths
Of night and light and the half-light,
I would spread the cloths under your feet:
But I, being poor, have only my dreams;
I have spread my dreams under your feet;
Tread softly because you tread on my dreams.

NO SECOND TROY

Why should I blame her that she filled my days
With misery, or that she would of late
Have taught to ignorant men most violent ways,
Or hurled the little streets upon the great,
Had they but courage equal to desire?
What could have made her peaceful with a mind
That nobleness made simple as a fire,
With beauty like a tightened bow, a kind
That is not natural in an age like this,
Being high and solitary and most stern?
Why, what could she have done, being what she is?
Was there another Troy for her to burn?

SHE MOVED THROUGH THE FAIR

My young love said to me, 'My brothers won't mind,
And my parents won't slight you for your lack of kind.'
Then she stepped away from me, and this she did say,
'It will not be long, love, till our wedding day.'

She stepped away from me and she moved through
    the fair,
And fondly I watched her go here and go there,
Then she went her way homeward with one star awake,
As the swan in the evening moves over the lake.

The people were saying no two were e'er wed
But one had a sorrow that never was said,
And I smiled as she passed with her goods and her gear,
And that was the last that I saw of my dear.

I dreamt it last night that my young love came in,
So softly she entered, her feet made no din;
She came close beside me, and this she did say,
'It will not be long, love, till our wedding day.'

ON RAGLAN ROAD
(Air: *The Dawning of the Day*)

On Raglan Road on an autumn day I met her first
    and knew
That her dark hair would weave a snare that I might
    one day rue;
I saw the danger, yet I walked along the enchanted way,
And I said, let grief be a fallen leaf at the dawning of
    the day.

On Grafton Street in November we tripped lightly
    along the ledge
Of the deep ravine where can be seen the worth of
    passion's pledge,
The Queen of Hearts still making tarts and I not
    making hay –
O I loved too much and by such by such is happiness
    thrown away.

I gave her gifts of the mind I gave her the secret sign
    that's known
To the artists who have known the true gods of sound
    and stone
And word and tint. I did not stint for I gave her poems
    to say.
With her own name there and her own dark hair like
    clouds over fields of May

On a quiet street where old ghosts meet I see her
    walking now
Away from me so hurriedly my reason must allow
That I had wooed not as I should a creature made
    of clay –
When the angel woos the clay he'd lose his wings at
    the dawn of day.

THE ARCHAEOLOGIST

Portrush. Walking dead streets in the dark.
Winter. A cold wind off the Atlantic
rattling metal in the amusement park.

Rain. The ornate dancehall, empty on the rocks,
bright paint worn thin, posters half torn away,
sweet-stalls, boarded up and locked with padlocks.

Returned to the scene, at once I see again
myself, when ten years younger, and a girl,
preserved in an almost perfect state by the brain.

That is her window, high on the side wall.
Beneath it figures, projected by the mind,
are moving. I am about to call.

I give her name and wait. She is called down.
Without taking thought I know what I want to do.
Love, like electric current, lights the town.

Nothing is tawdry, all our jokes are funny,
the pin-table is brighter than Shakespeare's works,
my handful of warm coins is sufficient money.

Imaginative reconstruction shed
some light upon a vanished way of life.
I cannot live like them, and they are dead.

The cold makes me simpler and breaks the spell:
I don't mind crying, but I hate to shiver,
and walk quickly back to my hotel.

THE HAULIER'S WIFE MEETS JESUS
ON THE ROAD NEAR MOONE

I live in the town of Cahir
In the Glen of Aherlow,
Not far from Peekaun
In the townland of Toureen,
At the foot of Galtee Mór
In the County of Tipperary.
I am thirty-three years old,
In the prime of my womanhood:
The mountain stream of my sex
In spate and darkly foaming;
The white hills of my breasts
Brimful and breathing;
The tall trees of my eyes
Screening blue skies;
Yet in each palm of my hand
A sheaf of fallen headstones.
When I stand in profile
Before my bedroom mirror
With my hands on my hips in my slip,
Proud of my body,
Unashamed of my pride,
I appear to myself a naked stranger,
A woman whom I do not know
Except fictionally in the looking-glass,

Quite dramatically beautiful.
Yet in my soul I yearn for affection,
My soul is empty for the want of affection.
I am married to a haulier,
A popular and a wealthy man,
An alcoholic and a county councillor,
Father with me of four sons,
By repute a sensitive man and he is
Except when he makes love to me:
He takes leave of his senses,
Handling me as if I were a sack of gravel
Or a carnival dummy,
A fruit machine or a dodgem.
He makes love to me about twice a year;
Thereafter he does not speak to me for weeks,
Sometimes not for months.
One night in Cruise's Hotel in Limerick
I whispered to him: Please *take* me.
(We had been married five years
And we had two children.)
Christ, do you know what he said?
Where? Where do you want me to take you?
And he rolled over and fell asleep,
Tanked up with seventeen pints of beer.
We live in a Georgian, Tudor, Classical Greek,
Moorish, Spanish Hacienda, Regency Period,
Ranch House, Three-Storey Bungalow

On the edge of the edge of town:
'Poor Joe's Row'
The townspeople call it,
But our real address is 'Ronald Reagan Hill' –
That vulturous-looking man in the States.
We're about twelve miles from Ballyporeen
Or, as the vulture flies, about eight miles.
After a month or two of silence
He says to me: Wife, I'm sorry;
I know that we should be separated,
Annulled or whatever,
But on account of the clients and the neighbours,
Not to mention the children, it is plain
As a pikestaff we are glued to one another
Until death do us part.
Why don't you treat yourself
To a weekend up in Dublin,
A night out at the theatre:
I'll pay for the whole shagging lot.

There was a play on at the time
In the Abbey Theatre in Dublin
Called *The Gigli Concert*,
And, because I liked the name –
But also because it starred
My favourite actor, Tom Hickey –
I telephoned the Abbey from Cahir.

They had but one vacant seat left!
I was so thrilled with myself,
And at the prospect of Tom Hickey
In a play called *The Gigli Concert*
(Such a euphonious name for a play, I thought),
That one wet day I drove over to Clonmel
And I went wild, and I bought a whole new outfit.
I am not one bit afraid to say
That I spent all of £200 on it
(Not, of course, that Tom Hickey would see me
But I'd be seeing myself seeing Tom Hickey
Which would be almost, if not quite,
The very next best thing):
A long, tight-fitting, black skirt
Of Chinese silk,
With matching black jacket
And lace-frilled, pearl-white blouse;
Black fishnet stockings with sequins;
Black stiletto high-heeled shoes
Of pure ostrich leather.
I thought to myself – subconsciously, of course –
If I don't transpose to be somebody's *femme fatale*
It won't anyhow be for the want of trying.

Driving up to Dublin I began to daydream
And either at Horse & Jockey or Abbeyleix
I took a wrong turn and within a quarter of an hour

I knew I was lost. I stopped the car
And I asked the first man I saw on the road
For directions:
'Follow me' – he said – 'my name is Jesus:
Have no fear of me – I am a travelling actor.
We'll have a drink together in the nearby inn.'
It turned out we were on the road near Moone.
(Have you ever been to the Cross at Moone?
Once my children and I had a picnic at Moone
When they were little and we were on one
Of our Flight into Egypt jaunts to Dublin.
They ran round the High Cross round and round
As if it were a maypole, which maybe it is:
Figure carvings of loaves and fishes, lions and dolphins.
I drank black coffee from a thermos flask
And the children drank red lemonade
And they were wearing blue duffle coats with red scarves
And their small, round, laughing, freckled faces
Looked pointedly like the faces of the twelve apostles
Gazing out at us from the plinth of the Cross
Across a thousand years.
Only, of course, their father was not with us:
He was busy – busy being our family euphemism.
Every family in Ireland has its own family euphemism
Like a heraldic device or a coat of arms.)
Jesus turned out to be a lovely man,
All that a woman could ever possibly dream of:

Gentle, wild, soft-spoken, courteous, sad;
Angular, awkward, candid, methodical;
Humorous, passionate, angry, kind;
Entirely sensitive to a woman's world.
Discreetly I invited Jesus to spend the night with me –
Stay with me, the day is almost over and it is getting
     dark –
But he waved me aside with one wave of his hand,
Not contemptuously, but compassionately.
'Our night will come,' he smiled,
And he resumed chatting about my children,
All curiosity for their welfare and well-being.
It was like a fire burning in me when he talked to me.
There was only one matter I felt guilty about
And that was my empty vacant seat in the Abbey.
At closing time he kissed me on both cheeks
And we bade one another goodbye and then –
Just as I had all but given up hope –
He kissed me full on the mouth,
My mouth wet with alizarin lipstick
(A tube of Guerlain 4 which I've had for twelve years).
As I drove on into Dublin to the Shelbourne Hotel
I kept hearing his Midlands voice
Saying to me over and over, across the Garden of
     Gethsemane –
Our night will come.

Back in the town of Cahir,
In the Glen of Aherlow,
Not far from Peekaun
In the townland of Toureen,
At the foot of Galtee Mór
In the County of Tipperary,
For the sake of something to say
In front of our four sons
My husband said to me:
Well, what was Benjamino Gigli like?
Oh, 'twas a phenomenal concert!
And what was Tom Hickey like?
Miraculous – I whispered – miraculous.
Our night will come – he had smiled – our night
    will come.

PAUL DURCAN (1944–)

MAYFLY

Barometer of my moods today, mayfly,
Up and down one among a million, one
The same at best as the rest of the jigging mayflies,
One only day of May alive beneath the sun.

The yokels tilt their pewters and the foam
Flowers in the sun beside the jewelled water.
Daughter of the South, call the sunbeams home
To nest between your breasts. The kingcups
Ephemeral are gay gulps of laughter.

Gulp of yellow merriment; cackle of ripples;
Lips of the river that pout and whisper round the reeds.
The mayfly flirting and posturing over the water
Goes up and down in the lift so many times for fun.

'When we are grown up we are sure to alter
Much for the better, to adopt solider creeds;
The kingcup will cease proffering his cup
And the foam will have blown from the beer and the
        heat no longer dance
And the lift lose fascination and the May
Change her tune to June but the trouble with us
        mayflies
Is that we never have the chance to be grown up.'

They never have the chance, but what of time they have
They stretch out taut and thin and ringing clear;
So we, whose strand of life is not much more,
Let us too make our time elastic and
Inconsequently dance above the dazzling wave.

Nor put too much on the sympathy of things,
The dregs of drink, the dried cups of flowers,
The pathetic fallacy of the passing hours
When it is we who pass them – hours of stone,
Long rows of granite sphinxes looking on.

It is we who pass them, we the circus masters
Who make the mayflies dance, the lapwings lift their
        crests;
The show will soon shut down, its gay-rags gone,
But when this summer is over let us die together,
I want always to be near your breasts.

LOUIS MacNEICE (1907–63)

ON NOT BEING YOUR LOVER

Your eyes were ever brown, the colour
of time's submissiveness. Love nerves
or a heart beat in their world of
privilege. I had not yet kissed you
on the mouth.

But I would not say, in my un-freedom
I had weakly drifted there, like the
bone-deep blue that visits and decants
the eyes of our children:

How warm and well-spaced their dreams
you can tell from the sleep-late mornings
taken out of my face! Each lighted
window shows me cardiganed, more desolate
than the garden, and more hallowed
than the hinge of the brass-studded
door that we close, and no one opens,
that we open and no one closes.

In a far-flung, too young part,
I remembered all your slender but
persistent volume said, friendly, complex
as the needs of your new and childfree girl.

226 MEDBH McGUCKIAN (1950–)

& FORGIVE US OUR TRESPASSES

Of which the first is love. The sad, unrepeatable fact
that the loves we shouldn't foster burrow faster and
    linger longer
than sanctioned kinds can. Loves that thrive on
    absence, on lack
of return, or worse, on harm, are unkillable, Father.
They do not die in us. And you know how we've tried.
Loves nursed, inexplicably, on thoughts of sex,
a return to touched places, a backwards glance,
    a sigh –
they come back like the tide. They are with us at
    the terminus
when cancer catches us. They have never been away.
Forgive us the people we love – their dragnet influence.
Those disallowed to us, those who frighten us, those
    who stay
on uninvited in our lives and every night revisit us.
Accept from us the inappropriate
by which our dreams and daily scenes stay separate.

COME LIVE WITH ME

Come live with me and be my mate
and all the fittings and the fixtures of the flat
will bust with joy –

                this flowered ottoman, this tallboy.
I'll leave a water-ring around your heart.
In the mildewed kitchenette of afternoon
TV, my cup of coffee
overfloweth. *Neighbours. Ironside.*
Whatever Happened to Baby Jane?
– that well-known scene in which, as you explain, the
      feral heel
Of Bette Davis meets Ms Crawford's head – head on –
      for real! for real!

INDEX OF FIRST LINES

ACKNOWLEDGMENTS

Thanks are due to the following copyright holders for permission to reprint:

SAMUEL BECKETT: 'Gnome' from *Collected Poems in English and French*, copyright © 1977 by Samuel Beckett. Used by permission of Grove/Atlantic, Inc. 'Gnome' from *Collected Poems of Samuel Beckett*. Reprinted with permission of Faber and Faber Limited. EAVAN BOLAND: 'In Her Own Image' Copyright © 1980 by Eavan Boland, 'Nocturne' Copyright © 1987 by Eavan Boland, 'Night Feed' Copyright © 1982 by Eavan Boland, from *An Origin Like Water: Collected Poems 1967–1987* by Eavan Boland. Used by permission of W. W. Norton & Company, Inc. 'In Her Own Image', 'Nocturne' and 'Night Feed' by Eavan Boland, from *New Collected Poems* by Eavan Boland. Used by permission of Carcanet Press Limited. COLETTE BRYCE: 'The Full Indian Rope Trick' taken from *The Full Indian Rope Trick* by Colette Bryce. © Colette Bryce, 2004. Reprinted with permission from Pan Macmillan, London. CIARAN CARSON: 'Belfast Confetti', 'Turn Again' and 'The Exiles' Club' by Ciaran Carson. By kind permission of the author and The Gallery Press, Loughcrew, Oldcastle, County Meath, Ireland, from *Collected Poems* (2008). Ciaran Carson: 'Belfast Confetti',

'Turn Again' and 'The Exiles' Club' from *Collected Poems*. Reprinted with permission from Wake Forest University Press. AUSTIN CLARKE: 'Penal Law' by Austin Clarke, from *Austin Clarke Collected Poems*, edited by R. Dardis Clarke, published by Carcanet Press/The Bridge Press (2008). Permission has been granted by R. Dardis Clarke, 17 Oscar Square, Dublin 8. DENIS DEVLIN: 'Ank'hor Vat' from *Collected Poems* by Denis Devlin, published by The Dedalus Press, 1989. Reprinted with permission from The Dedalus Press. www.dedaluspress.com PAUL DURCAN: 'The Haulier's Wife Meets Jesus on the Road Near Moone' by Paul Durcan. Reprinted with permission from Paul Durcan. PETER FALLON: 'The Herd' by Peter Fallon. By kind permission of the author and The Gallery Press, Loughcrew, Oldcastle, County Meath, Ireland, from *News of the World* (1998). LEONTIA FLYNN: 'Come Live With Me' from *These Days* by Leontia Flynn, published by Jonathan Cape. Reprinted by permission of The Random House Group Ltd. ALAN GILLIS: 'Progress' and 'The Ulster Way' by Alan Gillis. By kind permission of the author and The Gallery Press, Loughcrew, Oldcastle, County Meath, Ireland, from *Somebody, Somewhere* (2004). MICHAEL HARTNETT: 'There Will Be a Talking' by Michael Hartnett. By kind permission of the Estate of Michael Hartnett and The Gallery Press, Loughcrew, Oldcastle, County Meath, Ireland, from

Collected Poems (2001). SEAMUS HEANEY: Excerpt (30 lines) from 'The Cure at Troy' by Seamus Heaney. Reprinted with permission from Faber and Faber Limited. 60 lines of 'Whatever You Say Say Nothing', 'Anahorish', 'Mid-Term Break', 'Clearances III', 'Punishment', 'The Underground' and 'Requiem for the Croppies' from *Opened Ground* by Seamus Heaney. Reprinted with permission from Faber and Faber Limited. Excerpt (30 lines) from 'The Cure at Troy' by Seamus Heaney, and 60 lines of 'Whatever You Say Say Nothing', 'Anahorish', 'Mid-Term Break', 'Clearances III', 'Punishment', 'The Underground' and 'Requiem for the Croppies' from *Opened Ground* by Seamus Heaney. Reprinted with permission from Farrar, Straus & Giroux. JOHN HEWITT: An extract from 'The Lonely Heart' from 'Freehold' by John Hewitt. John Hewitt, *The Selected Poems of John Hewitt*, ed. Michael Longley and Frank Ormsby (Blackstaff Press, 2007), reproduced by permission of Blackstaff Press on behalf of the Estate of John Hewitt. PATRICK KAVANAGH: 'Memory of My Father', 'Prelude', 'Epic' and 'On Raglan Road' by Patrick Kavanagh. The poems by Patrick Kavanagh are reprinted from *Collected Poems*, edited by Antoinette Quinn (Allen Lane, 2004), by kind permission of the Trustees of the Estate of the late Katherine B. Kavanagh, through the Jonathan Williams Literary Agency. THOMAS KINSELLA: 'Chrysalides' by Thomas Kinsella, taken from *Selected Poems 1956–1968* (Dolmen Press, 1973). Reprinted with the kind permission of Thomas Kinsella. Excerpt from 'The Passing of the Poets' by Fear Flatha Ó Gnímh, translated by Thomas Kinsella, and 'For the Family of Cúchonnacht Ó Dálaigh' by Dáibhí Ó Bruadair, translated by Thomas Kinsella. Reprinted with the kind permission of Thomas Kinsella. NICK LAIRD: 'Poetry' from *To a Fault* by Nick Laird. Copyright © 2005 by Nick Laird. Used by permission of W. W. Norton & Company, Inc. 'Poetry' from *To a Fault* by Nick Laird. Reprinted with permission from Faber and Faber Limited. MICHAEL LONGLEY: 'In Memoriam'/'The Linen Industry' from *Collected Poems* by Michael Longley, published by Jonathan Cape. Reprinted by permission of The Random House Group Ltd. 'In Memoriam' and 'The Linen Industry'. Reprinted with permission from Wake Forest University Press. LOUIS MACNEICE: 'Snow', 'Wolves', 'Belfast', 'Mayfly' and 'Dublin' (stanza from 'The Closing Album') by Louis MacNeice, taken from *Collected Poems* (Faber, 1966). Reprinted with permission from David Higham Associates, London. DEREK MAHON: 'A Disused Shed in Co. Wexford' and 'Glengormley' by Derek Mahon. By kind permission of the author and The Gallery Press, Loughcrew, Oldcastle, County Meath, Ireland, from *Collected Poems* (1999). THOMAS MCCARTHY: 'The Standing Trains' is taken from *Mr Dineen's Careful*

Parade: New and Selected Poems by Thomas McCarthy. Published by Anvil Press Poetry in 1999. MEDBH MCGUCKIAN: 'The Sitting', 'On Not Being Your Lover', 'The "Singer"' and 'The Flower Master' by Medbh McGuckian. By kind permission of the author and The Gallery Press, Loughcrew, Oldcastle, County Meath, Ireland, from *Selected Poems* (1997). JOHN MONTAGUE: 'Like dolmens round my childhood, the old people', and '11 rue Daguerre' by John Montague. By kind permission of the author and The Gallery Press, Loughcrew, Oldcastle, County Meath, Ireland, from *Collected Poems* (1995). John Montague: 'Like dolmens round my childhood, the old people', and '11 rue Daguerre' from *Collected Poems*. Reprinted with permission from Wake Forest University Press. SINEAD MORRISSEY: '& Forgive Us Our Trespasses' from *Between Here and There* by Sinead Morrissey (Carcanet Press, 2002). Reprinted with permission from Carcanet Press Limited. PAUL MULDOON: 'Lunch with Pancho Villa', 'Quoof', 'Cuba' and 'Anseo' from *New Selected Poems* by Paul Muldoon. Reprinted with permission from Faber and Faber Limited. 'Symposium' from *Hay* by Paul Muldoon. Reprinted with permission from Faber and Faber Limited. 'Lunch with Pancho Villa', 'Quoof', 'Cuba' and 'Anseo' from *New Selected Poems* by Paul Muldoon. 'Symposium' from *Hay* by Paul Muldoon. Reprinted with permission from Farrar, Straus &

Giroux. RICHARD MURPHY: 'Seals at High Island' taken from *High Island* by Richard Murphy. Copyright © Richard Murphy. Reprinted with permission from Aitken Alexander Associates Limited. EILÉAN NÍ CHUIL-LEANÁIN: 'Deaths and Engines' by Eiléan Ní Chuil-leanáin. By kind permission of the author and The Gallery Press, Loughcrew, Oldcastle, County Meath, Ireland, from *Selected Poems* (2008). 'London' and 'So She Looked, in that Company' by Eiléan Ní Chuil-leanáin. By kind permission of the author and The Gallery Press, Loughcrew, Oldcastle, County Meath, Ireland, from *The Magdalene Sermon* (1989). Eiléan Ní Chuilleanáin: 'Deaths and Engines' from *The Second Voyage*, 'London' and 'So She Looked, in that Company' from *The Magdalene Sermon*. Reprinted with permission from Wake Forest University Press. NUALA NÍ DHOMH-NIALL: 'Miraculous Grass' by Nuala Ní Dhomhnaill, translated by Seamus Heaney. By kind permission of the author and The Gallery Press, Loughcrew, Oldcastle, County Meath, Ireland, from *Pharaoh's Daughter* (1990). MÁIRE CRUISE O'BRIEN (translator): 'My Son, Forsake Your Art' by Mathghamlain Ó Hifearnáin, translated by Máire Cruise O'Brien. Reprinted with the permission of Máire Cruise O'Brien. SÉAN Ó RÍORDÁIN: 'Claustropho-bia' by Séan Ó Ríordáin, translated by Patrick Crotty. Reprinted with the kind permission of Patrick Crotty. TOM PAULIN: 'Desertmartin' from *Liberty Tree* by Tom